8√1112
12

£9 -

INNOVATION THROUGH RECESSION

D0495832

UNIVERSITY OF S:

Please return *this book*
with it ar

!NNOVAT!ON through RECESS!ON

Edited by Geoffrey Squires

SOCIETY FOR RESEARCH INTO HIGHER EDUCATION

603470

UNIVERSITY OF
SUSSEX LIBRARY

Research into Higher Education Proceedings

The Society for Research into Higher Education
At the University, Guildford, Surrey GU2 5XH

First published 1983

© 1983 Society for Research into Higher Education

ISBN 0 900868 98 8

Printed in England by Direct Design (Bournemouth) Ltd. Printers
Butts Pond Industrial Estate, Sturminster Newton,
Dorset DT10 1AZ

CONTENTS

OVERVIEW
1 Innovation through Recession   1
  Geoffrey Squires   University of Hull

INNOVATIONS IN THE SYSTEM
2 Keynote Address: Knowledge, Work and Continuing Education   8
  Donald Bligh   University of Exeter
3 Contract Research in Higher Education   19
  Brian Salter   University of Surrey
4 The Education Counselling and Credit Transfer Information Service   28
  Peter Toyne   North East London Polytechnic
5 Structural Barriers to Innovation in West Germany   37
  Friedemann Schmithals   University of Bielefeld
6 Recession, Unemployment and Students in Germany   43
  *Götz Schindler   Bayerisches Statsinstitut für Hochschulforschung und
  Hochschulplanung*

INNOVATIONS IN INSTITUTIONS
7 A Marketing Perspective   46
  J.G. Duncan   Queen Margaret College, Edinburgh
8 Flexibility in Course Planning   56
  Eric Hewton   University of Sussex
9 Auditing Staff Energy   61
  *Graham J. Stodd   Bishop Otter College, West Sussex Institute of
  Higher Education*
10 Pathfinding Evaluation   66
  G.M.E. Blom and J.M. Verbeek   University of Amsterdam
11 Staff Development: a Case Study on Stress   78
  Anne Castling   College of Arts and Technology, Newcastle-upon-Tyne
12 Staff Development and Innovation Theory   85
  *Desmond Rutherford and Haydn Mathias   University of Birmingham
  and University of Southampton*

INNOVATIONS IN TEACHING
13 Student Self-Assessment   93
  *David Boud and Jacqueline Lublin   University of New South Wales
  and University of Sydney*
14 Cost-Effectiveness in Laboratory Teaching   100
  Lewis Elton   University of Surrey
15 Recession and Innovation in Sweden   108
  *Staffan Wahlen   National Board for Universities and Colleges,
  Stockholm*
16 The Potential of Educational Technology   112
  Norman Willis   Council for Educational Technology

17 Technology and the Resources Paradox   118
    Nick Rushby   Imperial College, London

    CONCLUSION
18 Three Innovation Strategies   123
    Geoffrey Squires   University of Hull

SRHE Annual Conference 1982 'Innovation through Recession'
CONFERENCE COMMITTEE MEMBERS

Ron Barnett, CNAA; Malcolm Cornwall, Brighton Polytechnic; Harriet Greenaway, Bristol Polytechnic; Eric Hewton (chairman), University of Sussex; Haydn Mathias, University of Southampton; John Richardson, Brunel University; Geoffrey Squires, University of Hull.

1 INNOVATION THROUGH RECESSION

Geoffrey Squires   University of Hull

At first sight, the recession in higher education, with which SRHE's 1982 annual conference was concerned, appears to be a purely economic phenomenon. Governments in the western industrialized countries, faced with what is now turning out to be not only a severe, but also a prolonged decline in economic activity, have on the whole responded with deflationary policies, involving increased taxes or cuts in public spending, or both. Even France, which under the new Mitterrand administration appeared to plan to spend its way out of the recession, is now beginning to backtrack. Changes of government in Norway and more recently in West Germany, as well as major economic uncertainty in Ireland, suggest that, in these countries too, some cuts in public spending are likely. Such cuts have already been made in Sweden and Holland, though not as severely as in the United Kingdom. Since one long-term trend in higher education in virtually all the western industrialized countries has been increased dependence upon state funding, the effect of these cuts on higher education has been much more severe than it would have been in the past.

As well as reduced government spending on higher education, there has been in some countries a reduction in private spending as well. The demand for higher education is influenced by a number of factors, and the situation is a complex one. Insofar as higher education is a form of consumption, recession and reduced spending power affect it just as they affect other consumable services. Moreover, the countervailing belief that higher education is a form of investment for the individual student has been shaken by increases in graduate unemployment, and by suspicion of a decline in the private rate of return. There is evidence in France, Germany, Italy, and Sweden of students hedging their bets between higher education and employment, preferring to do both part-time, officially or unofficially, or alternating education and employment in a recurrent pattern. They reduce their commitment to their studies because their studies have reduced benefits. It is not so much a matter of reduced demand for higher education as one of qualified or partial demand.

In the United Kingdom, where youth unemployment is now a severe problem, and where both educational and employment regulations make it difficult to combine study and work, students seem to have responded to the recession more by differentiating between subjects, and choosing those which seem to have more vocational value. This is however a risky business, since it involves predicting the job market several years hence. The alternative of keeping one's options open through a broad-based general degree is largely precluded by the specialized pattern of studies on which most institutions insist.

MULTIPLE DEMANDS
Economic factors thus seem to account for much of the recession in higher education. Insofar as these factors tend to be international, this at least means that people concerned with higher education from different countries have more in common to talk about than they usually do, a fact which is reflected in this volume of the

conference proceedings. However, the recession in higher education is more complex than the above account would suggest. Systems in many countries are being faced with a number of often conflicting demands from governments, from employers, from students, and not least from academics themselves. To begin with, there is the demand that institutions of higher education should continue to conduct research, especially what the OECD calls 'strategic research', which might provide the basis for a new industrial revolution through developments in information technology and biotechnology, and which might enable the industrialized countries to avoid competition with developing countries and to retain a position of relative advantage in the world economy. However, research tends to be expensive. If one tries to concentrate it in centres of excellence, one begins to formalize a hierarchy among institutions to which many academics would object. Centres of excellence might quickly become centres of orthodoxy. Moreover, the strength of individual departments waxes and wanes over time.

There is also the demand that research should be relevant and client-orientated, a demand embodied in the 'contract principle'. Unfortunately, research is by definition a rather unpredictable business, and efforts to subject it to long-term policies or short-term objectives are not always very successful. It may need to be 'over-funded' to some extent to counteract the hazards involved; and in many cases it requires continuity, a permanent platform from which to operate. Neither of these requirements accords well with economy.

Another demand placed on higher education systems is that they should produce more employable graduates, and put greater emphasis upon vocational subjects (that is, produce more engineers, accountants, or computer specialists, and fewer anthropologists, historians, or fine arts graduates). In the United Kingdom, the shift of emphasis from education to training is most marked in non-advanced further education, where the growth of the influence of the Manpower Services Commission has been dramatic. But the pressure is there too in higher education, in more discreet and less effective ways, and it appears to signal a firm policy distinction between vocational and non-vocational studies, between education-as-investment and education-as-consumption. The vocational/non-vocational distinction, however, breaks down in one crucial area, that of general education or generic training. Many jobs demand not so much technical expertise as general skills related to problem solving, human relationships, information handling, and evaluation. Such skills may form part of the process of studying a wide range of subjects, a process which is sometimes described in a short-hand way as 'learning to think' or 'developing one's mind'. Even Becker's *Human Capital* justified general education on economic grounds, on the basis that the job market always needs and can absorb a large number of generalists. Exactly what kind of generalist is another question; and perhaps we need to rethink our concept of generality in terms of contemporary culture and knowledge.

There are also various kinds of social demands placed on higher education. Chief among these is that higher education should provide an opportunity to all who can benefit from it to develop their knowledge and skills; that it should be a right, either statutory as in some continental countries, or effective as in the English-speaking countries. But it is also still quite widely felt (as was shown by SRHE's 1981 annual conference, which dealt with bias in higher education) that higher education should be equitable; that its recipients should be representative of the population as a whole, in terms of social class, sex, race, region, and age, and even that it should help to redress inequalities by positive discrimination. On the matter of social class there is now some disillusionment: a feeling that the crucial educational choices are made much earlier in a person's life; but the proportions of women and mature students in the system have increased over the last two decades in many countries. Race, a major issue in American higher education, is only beginning to be discussed in a European context. There is also the demand that institutions of higher education should relate to and contribute to their local communities to a greater extent than they have in the past, without however losing their status as part of a national or international system. The notion of the 'service' institution has gained ground.

Then there are the rather diffuse demands for flexibility and responsiveness. It is commonly felt that systems of higher education should be less rigid in terms of access, transfer, and the format and content of courses. There should be more paths into and through higher education, and fewer obstacles and dead-ends. Moreover, it is felt that institutions should (in some ill-defined way) be more 'responsive', either to the needs of society or to the needs of their students. The concept of 'needs' here is a slippery one, but what probably lies behind the call for responsiveness is the idea that institutions of higher education have in the past been too subject-centred and too dominated by their own internal priorities, and have thus tended to produce graduates very much in their own image, miniature academics. For example, a recent SRHE Leverhulme seminar called roundly for teaching to be more 'student-centred' (Bligh, D.A. (Editor) (1982) *Accountability or Freedom for Teachers?* and *Professionalism and Flexibility in Learning* Guildford: SRHE).

Finally, there is the demand that quality should be maintained. Like 'needs', 'quality' is an elusive notion. Privately, lecturers will usually admit that some institutions, and certainly some departments, are better than others. Admissions grades, staff qualifications, and research output are cited as measures (albeit indirect) of 'quality'. However, what often strikes foreigners looking at the United Kingdom system is the relative overall consistency of quality in higher education: the fact that in a sizeable system a generally high standard is maintained, partly through selective admissions policies, and partly through the supervision of the polytechnics by the Council for National Academic Awards and through the self-policing of the universities. When people demand that quality should be maintained, they are probably asking that we maintain the useful fiction of comparability or parity between institutions and sectors of higher education. But quality has another aspect, also often noticed by outsiders: the fact that, by and large, students in the United Kingdom are cared for and treated as individuals. The favourable (by international standards) staff/student ratios, the tradition of tutorial help, the whole apparatus of counselling and care, all point to the 'quality of care' in higher education, and this again is something that many people would be loath to see eroded, perhaps out of nostalgia for some collegial ideal.

The demands placed upon higher education at present are, therefore, multiple and sometimes conflicting. If it were simply a matter of cutting costs, that could probably be done quite quickly and even simply. Student numbers could be reduced drastically; loans substituted for grants; most institutions required to have a 75% local intake; cheap subjects encouraged; institutions closed down or scaled up to 'economic size'; research concentrated in a 'super-league'; staff/student ratios doubled; mass teaching methods introduced. The initial investment necessary to bring about such changes (mainly in the form of redundancy payments and new technology) could possibly be recouped within a few years. But the real problem in higher education policy, as in so many other policy areas, is that of achieving the best balance or trade-off between multiple desirable ends, and cost-effectiveness is only one of these. The above changes would alter the current system of higher education out of all recognition, not only in form and substance, but in the basic mechanisms of regulation and control.

Thus, attempts to innovate during or in response to the current recession take place within a delicate ecology of multiple objectives, often related and sometimes conflicting; and this book (papers submitted to the 1982 SRHE annual conference) bears witness to that ecology without exception. Innovation in higher education has never been easy; the complex organizational patterns, the delicate balance between bureaucracy and collegiality and between central planning and local government ensure it, even if nothing else does. But in the past some innovators thought that it was easier to innovate than it actually was, and boldly proclaimed new curricula, new kinds of institutions, new technologies, and so on. The innovations described and discussed in this book are sadder and wiser; there is a sense both of the need to change and of the difficulty in achieving change. Three main levels of innovation need to be distinguished: innovations at the central, policy-making level; innovations in the organization and management of educational institutions; and innovations in curricula and teaching. The book is concerned, deliberately, with the second and third of these, and most of the papers are therefore related to either organizational or pedagogical questions, or a mixture of the two. However, since the policies of central government are typically more interventionist than they used to be, and tend to pervade both organizational and pedagogical issues, most papers refer to them in passing, and some discuss them directly.

INNOVATIONS IN THE SYSTEM
All the papers in the first section of this volume of proceedings address macro, system-wide issues. Bligh (Chapter 2) is concerned above all with the curriculum and the structures that are needed to carry it. He proposes major changes both in the content and organization of post-school education, leading to a broader, more flexible, and recurrent system. Underlying his reconstruction of the institution is a reconstruction of the map of knowledge.

Salter (Chapter 3) is concerned with that other major function of higher education, research. From a detailed analysis of trends in research expenditure and employment, he comes to the conclusion that higher education's position as a research base is now dangerously exposed, and that a 'cycle of deprivation' is operating in the area of short-term research posts.

Toyne, more optimistically, (Chapter 4) traces the development of interest in credit transfer and counselling, a development which has now reached the stage of a pilot operation in the south-west. He argues that the widespread adoption of credit-based courses would affect not only the relationship between institutions, but the very structure of higher education curricula, raising questions to do with the optimum length and breadth of degree courses.

The two other papers in this section, by Schmithals and Schindler, taken together (Chapter 5 and 6), give an interesting account of the current need for, and historical constraints on, innovation in West Germany. In some respects, continental governments seem to have more bureaucratic control over higher education than in the United Kingdom, and attempts to innovate from the bottom up can run into bureaucratic obstacles. On the other hand, bureaucracies can also attempt to impose innovations themselves, with, as Schmithals shows, varying degrees of success. In the United Kingdom, by contrast, the levers have tended to be purely monetary ones, consisting of straightforward cuts in resources with rather broad hints about priorities. The papers from the United Kingdom tend to grapple, therefore, not so much with bureaucracy as with economic stringency coupled with policy secrecy.

INNOVATIONS IN INSTITUTIONS
Innovations in the organization and management of institutions can point outwards, to changes in the relationships between the institution and its environment, or inwards, to internal structures and processes. The paper by Duncan (Chapter 7) falls into the first category. He suggests that institutions of higher education might market themselves more self-consciously, and he discusses how this might be done and what problems they might encounter. The idea that higher education exists in a market at all is something rather new in the United Kingdom; it may be symptomatic of uncertainties about the traditional eighteen-year-old intake (resulting from a combination of demography and demand), a new awareness of the potential adult market and the effects of government cutbacks and quotas upon certain categories of students.

The papers by Hewton, Stodd, Blom and Verbeek, Castling and Rutherford and Mathias (Chapter 8-12) all look inward at the internal problems of organization and management which arise in recession. Hewton examines the curent method of costing courses, which tends to pronounce small courses uneconomic, thereby leading to their closure. He suggests an alternative model, based upon institutional earnings per student. Stodd explores ways of arriving at a total audit of staff energy, so that limited staff resources can be used more effectively. This is a clear, if still rather general, response to economic pressures. Blom and Verbeek expound the notion of 'pathfinding evaluation' which goes beyond the evaluation of specific courses to explore and develop an overall identity and policy for a department. They show convincingly how this can enhance a department's chances of survival and growth in the medium term. Castling describes some of the human consequences of such pressures, in terms of stress and lack of communication among academic staff, and the response to such problems in one particular institution. Since staff not only account for the largest proportion (typically 75%) of the costs of institutions, but also constitute their main resource, such studies are very welcome. If a service or sector is labour-intensive, as higher education is, it is only sensible to think hard about the quality, morale, motivation, and experience of that labour force. The discussion of the 'new blood' problem in British universities shows some belated recognition of that fact, even though the implicit metaphor is less than human. Finally, Rutherford and Mathias relate staff development to innovation theory, and argue that some headway can be made, provided that developers are sensitive to the peculiar characteristics of higher education.

INNOVATIONS IN TEACHING
The third level of innovation is that of curriculum, teaching, assessment, and related activities. In one way, one would expect the curriculum — what people actually teach and learn — to be the core issue in higher education. However, as with many other conferences on higher education, the remaining papers selected here from the SRHE conference do not direct much attention towards this area. In British higher education there are three main patterns of curriculum: the specialized Honours degree, with its sub-type, joint Honours; the professionally orientated degree, either sandwich or non-sandwich; and the (relatively) open-choice modular degree. Major issues arise in all three of these. What is the optimum combination of (or balance between) specialization and generality, theory and practice, prescription and

negotiation? Is the policy shift from education to training which was mentioned earlier educationally desirable? Is it even economically desirable? How far does a 'new clientele' for higher education entail new curricula? What is the status of interdisciplinary courses? Do modular systems alter our whole conception of knowledge? Why do specialist departments tend to re-emerge? And so on. It is regrettable that there are no papers here specifically addressed to such questions, some of which are raised in the earlier papers by Bligh and Toyne.

Finally, there are innovations in teaching and assessment. These seem to take two general forms: first, a shift of responsibility from teachers to students; and second, a shift from teachers to technology. The arguments for the first tend to be both educational and economic; it would cost less if students taught themselves more, but it would also be educationally desirable because intellectual autonomy is a widely agreed objective of higher education. Boud and Lublin's paper (Chapter 13) on student self-assessment invokes both of these rationales. The thesis of Elton's paper (Chapter 14), while referring to the new technology, does not in fact depend upon it; he shows that cost-effectiveness in laboratory teaching can be increased through a proper analysis of aims and concomitant evaluation in a system 'notorious for never having evaluated its own operation'. Wahlen (Chapter 15) argues that budget cuts may be compensated for by changes which lead to more effective use of student time; his particular example is drawn from the English Department at Stockholm University.

Educational technology has had several false dawns, but the time has now perhaps arrived when it can have a major impact on teaching and learning, and Willis argues this case (Chapter 16), citing examples of a range of innovations in a variety of institutions. Rushby (Chapter 17) examines the role that the new technology might play in cutting costs, giving four examples: word processing, teleconferencing, information retrieval, and computer-based learning.

CONCLUSIONS

The recession in higher education has been not only an economic recession, but also a recession of hope. There was a general belief in higher education in the 1960s: a conviction that it helped bring about economic growth; that it could make society more equitable and individuals' lives more fulfilled; that it was a right. Government, and perhaps too the general public, seem less convinced nowadays of the benefits of higher education, and just as it was fashionable in the 1960s to applaud it, it is fashionable now in some quarters to deride it. But behind such swings in fashion there is a longer-term problem of governments caught between limited or falling revenue, due to economic recession, and rising public expenditure. There is no room here to discuss the policy priorities within education, let alone between education and other sectors — health, welfare, defence, industrial investment. The basic fact is that government spending as a percentage of GDP has tended to rise in the United Kingdom and in many other countries, irrespective of the party in power, and certain trends (for example, in population structure, health needs, and unemployment) suggest that it will continue to rise in the future. What concerns us here is the response of those in higher education to this situation.

As we have sketched them out here, the complex demands placed upon the system entail a complex response. In different ways this is confirmed (even assumed) by all the contributors to this volume of conference papers. They do not offer simple, immediate panaceas. Moreover, they also suggest, in different ways, how higher education might benefit from being regarded not merely as being concerned with knowledge and research, but as being itself an object of knowledge and research. It is ridiculous that we spend so little money investigating an activity which costs so much, yet the results of this neglect are unsurprising: much policy and planning which is entirely ad hoc in nature, and much organization and teaching which is based solely on habit.

Innovation goes on in higher education all the time. Courses change, research alters the map of knowledge, institutions evolve. Much of this innovation is not recognized as such, partly because it is correctly believed to be part of the normal state of affairs, and partly because most academics perceive educational innovation as being marginal to their central aims or interests. However, the problems now facing higher education seem to demand another order of change: not expansion, which is easy; nor simply contraction, which is painful; but adaptation, which is difficult; adaptation of both objective structures and subjective norms and attitudes. It is perhaps in the second rather than the first that the real problem of innovation lies.

2   KEYNOTE ADDRESS: KNOWLEDGE, WORK AND CONTINUING EDUCATION

Donald Bligh   University of Exeter

The way out of recession is through a new approach to work and a new sense of community. These are the lessons to be learned from Japan and Germany; not to copy or to transplant their institutions. The twin themes of work and community run through this paper. In my opinion education in general, and higher education in particular, has had too little to do with either in the recent past.

OUR EDUCATIONAL HERITAGE

Our curricula and our academic departments still reflect the values of a pre-industrial age. The Industrial Revolution brought many new forms of work. The innovators were not men of letters but men of humble origin with little or no education. The reaction to the Industrial Revolution by nineteenth-century educationists such as Matthew Arnold was protective of the values of the past and fearful, rather than inquisitive, innovative, adaptive or exploitative. In Arnold's book *Culture and Anarchy* the world of work and technology is placed more on the side of anarchy than of culture.

The contrasting attitudes of the industrialists and the educationists led to very different ideas for curricula. Instead of welcoming technology for the opportunities it offered, the fearful reaction of the men of letters was to give a small space to the study of science without its application to work and technology and to implant it in a milky stew of nineteenth-century culture — the classics, history, poetry and literature. More important, the map of knowledge was divided into regions with minimal overlap and with more relevance to the life of a leisured gentleman than to the world of work. There was still a belief that just as the qualities of mind learned in the study of classics would transfer to decision making in the civil service, so an appreciation of the work of Wordsworth, Keats and Shelley would bring sensitivity and empathy in human affairs.

Orwell's view of 1984 was the same — fearful and protective of former values, rather than asking how new technologies could be used for the good of all. There was the same reaction to the two cultures debate in the late 1950s. By the early 1960s those of us teaching in further education were required to give trainee craft apprentices a weekly dollop of liberal studies. It was supposed to help them communicate. Students in the arts and languages department were *not* given a corresponding dollop of technology. They weren't even given science. The controllers of our educational values were, and still are, arts men. The technologists were too busy doing technology. There is a similar confused reaction today in the attitudes of many people to behaviourism and conditioning. They are feared as threats to our freedom not as insights to be used for the good of all.

If we go back to the nineteenth century again, even more influential so far as higher education was concerned were the ideas of the university set out by Cardinal Newman. He positively praised the rarified atmosphere of the university, the study of a subject for its own sake, and the irrelevance of its application. The citadel of the intellect was seen as having sublime value. Mechanistic, manual and practical occupations were relegated in esteem.

These values, this relegation and the subject boundaries, are still with us. Why? In 1917 the government gave responsibility for school-leaving examinations to the universities. In this way a circle of values was cemented. School curricula inevitably reflected the examinations, in particular the examinations for university entrance. I hardly need to expound how the curricula of trade and commerce were squeezed out, how technical schools were places for people not good enough to go to grammar school, how schools have become divorced from places of work, how most teachers have never had a job outside the educational system, how class divisions have been perpetuated, how so many children of secondary age have for generations loathed and rejected what schools have to offer, how these attitudes and skills in avoidance of work have too often transferred to the world of employment, and how employment is divided into workers and management like pupils and 'masters' at school.

Part of the responsibility for this fiasco lies with the universities, in their failure to innovate either through recession or out of it, in their over-concentration on things intellectual to the exclusion of other things and to a degree of imbalance that contradicts the values of balanced judgement which we claim to espouse. Consequently, reform of the examination system is one of the group of educational innovations that is essential if Britain is to come through its twentieth-century decline and recession.

My children have a toy which they call a weeble. It is a round bottomed man rather like Humpty Dumpty. It is weighted so that if you push it at the top it will swing to and fro in ever smaller swings until it comes to rest in exactly the same position as when you first applied pressure to it. For the purposes of my analogy this is an academic weeble. It is possible to spend a great amount of energy applying pressures to bring about innovations, and much of this kind has been done in the last twenty years, but in the end, after periods of alternating action and reaction, educational practice comes to rest almost exactly where it was before. The energy required to maintain innovations cannot be sustained unless you can apply the pressure at the right point. To do that you have to shift the system as a whole. Only when a sizeable pressure is applied to the centre of gravity of the system (not its base, its foundations — people are forever challenging fundamentals) can the whole thing be permanently shifted. Two things lie near the centre of gravity of the educational system: finance and validation. The examination system is one aspect of validation. In a time of recession, in a time of financial stringency, pressures are applied in the area of finance. Higher education as an end in itself, rather than an investment with a financial return, is no longer publicly acceptable.

It is not vocational training that is required. Far from it. It is the liberalizing influence of the world of work as well as leisure, 'liberalizing' because the world of work is incredibly diverse. A hundred years ago it was different. Work was monotonous then. Now, a perceptive understanding and experience of many different kinds of work broaden one's outlook, breathe life into embryonic skills and make possible an appreciation of the lives and feelings of others.

In education, the power of institutions, the centre, and consumers are constantly held in triangular tension. In higher education the centre may be the DES, the UGC, the Committee of Vice-Chancellors, the National Advisory Body, the regional advisory councils or whatever. The centre has three functions: finance, planning and validation. Ultimately, if not sooner, the first two must be vested in the same institution while validation is best done by a separate body. The consumers may be students or employers.

At the present time there is a shift of power away from the institutions and the students towards the centre and the employers. The Robbins principle gave students, qualified by ability and attainment, a strong expectation of entering higher education. Institutions controlled their curricula and had a high degree of autonomy. The gradual reassertion of the power of the centre since 1967 is obvious: consider for example the establishment of the polytechnics, the rise of the CNAA, the central finance of the Open University, the rapid expansion and closure of the colleges of education, the treatment of overseas students, the placement of the Manpower Services Commission and the Open Tech under the Department of Employment, the fiscal constraint of the early 1980s, and most recently the establishment of the National Advisory Body. I believe it is also right not that employers should have greater power, but that the world of work should have greater influence.

RECONSTRUCTION OF THE MAP OF KNOWLEDGE
To achieve this I believe there should be a fundamental reconstruction of the map of knowledge and skills under six broad faculties and that examinations from sixteen-plus and beyond should reflect these faculties. I am calling therefore for a fundamental reconstruction of our curricula.

It should be a basic principle that the curricula at any stage of education should reflect the needs of those people leaving the educational system at that stage. In particular the curricula of secondary schools should reflect the needs of the vast majority of children for places of employment at the age of sixteen. We have, in my opinion, ignored the very powerful influence of higher education curricula upon school curricula for too long. I believe that in the past this influence has not always been for the good.

Schools have adapted their curricula to the demands of higher education, while the vast majority of young people neither obtain, nor seek entrance to higher education. The consequence has been that school curricula are unnecessarily abstract and theoretical and have thereby vitiated all the problems of motivation in the secondary school, which more occupationally oriented courses might have avoided. Furthermore, a greater emphasis at the school level upon the wide variety of skills required in employment could lay the foundation for the problem solving and the higher mental skills that we seek, while the present system encourages factual memory and regurgitation. I therefore want to design a system of examination, selection and curricula which will assume a different kind of secondary education and upon which higher education will be better able to build.

Communication
This is a large and wide-ranging faculty including English and foreign languages, art, graphic design, film and music; but I'm not necessarily suggesting that these things should be taught under these headings. This faculty is concerned with powers of expression, and interpretation, mutual understanding and aesthetic appreciation. It includes rhetoric, the art of salesmanship: persuasion and the role of body language and non-verbal communication. It is essentially an activity between two or more people. It is not the passive study of literature. As much, or more time should be spent on the study of dramatic technique on television today as on Shakespeare's dramatic technique. I am not suggesting the two are separable; but I am less concerned with these things on the timetable than with the qualities of mind they employ. I am concerned with cultural understanding, listening and tolerance as much if not more than the hallowed authors in the history of English literature.

Communication is a practical activity, not something confined to classrooms as English and kindred disciplines usually are today. It is something to learn in shops, buses and places of work; and that is where, in part, it should be taught. We need to get away from the idea that education is something done by teachers. We learn to communicate from our family and from members of the community. The job of the teacher is to involve members of the community, not to try to do all the teaching himself. The education of the young is a community responsibility which teachers should be trained to manage.

Maths, Computing and Logic
I do not believe that I need to make out the case for the growing and vital importance of this faculty in the next fifty years. There is some evidence to suggest that the fundamental development of the mental skills involved takes place around the age of nine: too early perhaps for secondary, let alone higher educational curricula, to have much influence. Equally significant is an apparent decline in the ability to learn these skills after the age of twenty-five or thirty if they are not well practised earlier. Hence to maximize such skills in the young adult should be a major function of post-secondary and continuing education.

There is otherwise severe danger of a widening generation gap in an area of growing social importance. In places of employment, the dangers of senior management having a poor appreciation of computer literacy in the presence of frustrated and sophisticated junior staff can be imagined. Conversely, if junior staff are given their head, older colleagues who are bypassed will be frustrated, disenchanted and depressed for more than half their working life.

I am concerned with the emotional context of these subjects. They are feared by most people, and it will be increasingly critical in our society that they are not. In this connection it is in the interests of higher education, the world of work, the education by mothers of succeeding generations, and the development of our common culture for the twenty-first century that we do something to stop squandering a vast national resource — the mathematical, logical and computing abilities of girls. The age participation rate for girls in the public sector of higher education has declined from 8.1 in 1972/3 to 4.7 in 1978/9. This reflects the contraction of teacher training, but the question must be asked: What use is being made of these female resources now? If they have potential for higher education, what use is being made of that potential? I suspect the answer is none. If so, that is scandalous. The blame for that scandal does not lie solely with the Department of Education and Science. Does it not also show that higher education is not providing alternative courses that these potential students either want or could enter? True, a proportion of this diminished group cannot enter higher education elsewhere because they do not have 'A' levels, but 'A' levels are only a requisite because we are obsessed with the prestige of providing three and four-year degree-level courses and little else.

Similarly, the linguistic skills required by the essay examinations that dominate the gateways to higher education disproportionately exclude members of lower social classes who may have considerable and valuable competence in the fields of mathematics, logic and computing. The influence of Cardinal Newman and Matthew Arnold is still with us. We operate by a process of exclusion, not of seeking and cultivating intellectual talents as a scarce resource.

Health
This faculty includes medicine, biology, gardening, agriculture and physical education. Our present examination system at 16 + demands that students of biology

know all about spirogyra, but very little about the elementary principles of health care, what to do in an emergency, and how to cultivate one's garden. It is a comment upon our educational system that the level of instruction required by the recent safety at work act is so elementary. In no way do I denigrate the work of the St John's Ambulance; but the fact that the work is what it is, and not another thing, is also a comment upon the general level of health education in our society.

Members of the National Health Service occasionally enter our schools to check on which children have nits or bad teeth; it is rare for them to enter our schools to make a significant contribution to teaching. But why not? Why should the education of our children be so isolated from vital matters of life and death in our community? How many million working days lost each year could have been saved if our homes and our minds had been better prepared?

This faculty is not only concerned with those patterns of thinking which characterize the biological sciences, and whether they may, or may not, be different from the physical sciences. It is concerned with respect for life, including parks and forests as well as animal life. It is concerned to break down the barriers between the medical profession and the public, to remove the myths and ignorance about dieting, back pain, drugs and magic cures.

Engineering and Technology
This faculty includes the physical sciences, inquiry, invention and design. It is concerned with the use of scientific methods to solve problems. It is essential that the problems considered at secondary level should be manifestly applicable to the problems of everyday life. They should be problems concerned with car maintenance, architectural design, building construction, fire prevention, domestic electrical appliances, the use of materials, how to freeze foods, loading for transport, the principles of polishing, methods of washing, how to heat a building, human movement, the design of tools. ... I am appalled at my inability to repair my own car, or even to understand how much of it works. (It's a new Metro with low fuel consumption, low wind resistance, front wheel drive, etc. Each of these features, and many more, employ important physical and design principles.)

If the future of the British economy depends upon the ingenuity of her engineers and her designers, the education system should adapt to make their emergence more likely. Thus the problems we give our students must not be simply confined to those with one or two right answers, but must be problems to find out, problems to invent and to design. These are problems where there may be many possible answers. In other words we need to encourage the divergent thinking of our future engineers and technicians. (As Hudson and others have shown, they tend to be convergent in their thinking.)

Again, essential to this process is the involvement of members of the community in teaching. The motor mechanic, the architect, the builder, the fire prevention officer and the heating engineer all have their place in the process of teaching and learning. The job of the professional teacher is to co-ordinate and assist their contribution, to prepare the children for it, to follow it up and to place what the children do in a context.

Of course the teaching of all these things does not leave out the teaching of science as we now know it. It puts it in a context. If you invite a heating engineer into school, or better still take the pupils out on a job, they will need to learn certain principles of the expansion and convection of fluids. They will need to understand why you sometimes get air locked in the top of radiators, but they will learn it in the context of a practical job.

I'm well aware that the readers of this book are very used to dealing with abstractions and it may seem that I am unnecessarily labouring the point; but that, if I may say so, is the trouble. Our curricula have forever been designed and taught by intellectuals. They are too strongly influenced by the thought that we must first teach abstract general principles and memorize unrelated facts before those principles and facts can be applied to practical problems. The simple truth is, the less able our students are, the more important it is to teach these things the other way round: to raise practical problems from common experience first, and then to draw general principles from them. The extreme case lies in traditional medical curricula in which students spend three years mugging up facts classified as anatomy, physiology, biochemistry and then, on the assumption that they have perfect powers of recall, are expected to be able to apply this information, with little previous practice, to clinical circumstances. Along with McMaster University and Nottingham, Southampton has made a notable break from this tradition.

Decision Making

This is another very large faculty. It includes decisions in management, systems thinking, administration, environmental planning, home management, accountancy and ethics as well as what commonly passes for social studies, history, politics, sociology, industrial relations, law, organization and methods, and economics. Again, I am less concerned with these subjects as they now stand than with the distinctive intellectual processes by which decisions are made. These include the capacity to handle vast quantities of information simultaneously, analysis and synthesis of that information, intuition, judgement, powers of generalization and the application of principles. Particularly important, it includes searching all the knowledge one has at one's disposal, in contrast to the compartmentalism commonly encouraged by contemporary examinations and curricula. It involves the use of discussion, case studies, projects, work experience and generally much more enterprise in teaching methods than is commonly practised today. For example if we teach history as such, it should be taught more by asking 'what would you have done if you had been in Charles I's position after the battle of Naseby?' than by requiring the pupils to remember the succession of events. In other words, the conception of history as a series of decisions and the conception that we, too, are part of the historical process, seems to me to be commonly neglected.

Consider another example: the series of decisions on where you place pots, pans, basins, knives, food of different kinds and all the other contents of a kitchen. The people who design kitchens usually plan the distribution of furniture (the refrigerator, cooker, sink and so on); but they can't take the multitude of small decisions that in practice dominate many important daily activities. The consequences are more far reaching than we care to think. There *are* principles involved (eg items used frequently are usually best near to hand, associated items may be stored together, their position should not lead to strained backs or unnecessary waste of time) but how are these principles arrived at, and how many housewives are aware of them?

Personal Relations

As far as I can see, this faculty scarcely appears in the modern school curriculum, yet it is highly relevant to the lives of everyone. It includes the study of individual development, parenthood, career development, one's own and other people's education, family care and the interaction of individuals in groups. As in other faculties, I am less concerned with the factual knowledge about these subjects, than with the distinctive mental skills required. They include the problem of self-identity with which many of our students struggle at university. There is some development of emotional empathy, which the harshness of the inner city schools squashes out of our pupils, rather than cultivates. There is the ability to regard oneself objectively and to see oneself from many points of view. There are the powers of interpersonal perception which are so vital for a harmonious life both at home and at work. Too often we are defensive because we do not think other people can appreciate how we feel. If the study of personal relations became a more common part of everyday culture, our defensiveness, and many of the problems that arise from it, could be reduced.

INTER-DIGITATING EMPLOYMENT AND POST-SECONDARY EDUCATION

Although I think each of these faculties involves distinctive mental skills I am not trying to do the same job that Paul Hirst did seventeen years ago. The mental skills overlap and ought to. The first two are relatively fundamental cognitive abilities. The next two are analytical and more concerned with solving problems by the application of principles. The problems studied in decision making and in personal relations require more synthesis and draw upon the knowledge and skills learned in the other faculties. Of course, I recognize that the programme I have outlined more than doubles the size of the secondary curriculum, if you think about it in the terms of the facts to be taught. I also accept that it would not be possible to have an examination at 16 + consisting wholly of unseen problems. A substantial number of marks will continue to be for factual knowledge. But I wish to encourage a move in this direction.

You may be asking what has all this got to do with innovation in *higher* education. Of course changes in the curricula at school level will dramatically affect teaching and curricula in higher education, but what has this innovation to do with the recession apart from orienting children towards jobs they are unlikely to be able to get? The answer lies in a much more radical proposal to change the patterns of education and employment and to achieve the much needed revolution in continuing education.

We cannot come through the recession without changing our work force. Re-employment requires career change. We cannot achieve career change without recurrent or continuing education for that change. Consequently all post-secondary education, including higher education, will need to make a major adaptation to the needs of continuing education.

Let me spell out, a little more, the changes I envisage in the patterns of employment and education.

Employment

We need to establish a new pattern of work in which people have either one or two half-time jobs with the same or different employers. Such a pattern has long existed in some European countries. In this way we can reduce the ludicrous situation in which three million people are unemployed while at the same time another group are slogging their guts out earning ulcers and coronaries. We need to share the work and share the leisure. A further advantage of half-time is that more than half the amount of work gets done. Fatigue is less, partly because a change brings re-invigoration, and partly because those with only *one* half-time job give the best half of their working effort. You will remember that in some industries output actually increased during the three day week in 1974.

In the context of half-time work, there is one large section of the community which deserves far more attention and more of our educational resources: I mean mothers. Even without the principles of equal opportunity, important as they are, the increasing number of one-parent families means that women need to be able to earn a family wage. Mothers in their late twenties and early thirties must be able to build a career for themselves and that means we must create the necessary part-time training opportunities for them. We need greater facilities and greater commitment for this aspect of continuing education.

Once we can establish habits of half-time work and promote the half-time employment of women at a wage similar to their husbands, then, with the wife's earnings it will be possible to let the husband work half-time so that he can seize the opportunities of continuing education and retrain during the other half. In this way we can introduce flexibility and career change into our labour force. Without it, individuals must make large scarifices to undertake retaining, even for short periods, let alone three-year Honours degrees in residential institutions. With opportunities for career change, without major material sacrifice, workers need feel less protective of their jobs and less insistent on restrictive practices. Higher and continuing education make major contributions to these issues, but for too long we have sat in judgement on the sidelines and believed that education is neither implicated nor involved. These patterns of employment and education will go some way to achieving five major goals:

a   Increased social and occupational *mobility* through career change.
b   A widening diversity of *experience* in both education and work.
c   Increased educational *opportunity* — particularly providing adults with a second chance and providing flexible re-routing within the educational system itself. Credit transfer has its place here.
d   A fairer *distribution* of *employment* and wealth. Our present unemployment is morally wrong and practically inefficient.
e   Greater *production* through reduced fatigue.

The Importance of Continuing Education

There are other arguments for the importance of continuing education. Community education — continuing education — is essential to a democracy. In a democracy we have a moral obligation to promote powers of decision making and thought of all kinds in *all* members of the community. Ultimately their thought is sovereign. Ideas and knowledge are developing all the time; so the powers of the mind must also be promoted and developed all the time too.

It is no good telling a man of fifty-five that he had his opportunity to develop the powers of his mind forty years ago. Firstly, he didn't. Secondly, thought cannot be separated from its content (that's the myth of classics, again), and modern content is quite different. One function of teachers is to diversify the content of thought. This does not imply increasing the recommended reading lists, but teaching by sharing experience. Mass media presentations are too narrow to be the sole vehicles for the content of thought. Discussion is important too. I cannot stress too strongly that the growth of continuing education should herald a totally new *style* of higher education — more consultative in its practice, more considerate in its regulations and with more community involvement in its content. This means that the schools and colleges must teach the students of tomorrow to take much more responsibility for their own learning.

Another function of teachers in higher education is to cultivate a spirit of inquiry throughout the community. Why is it that the university ethos of inquiry — a searching for the truth — has not gone the way of academic drift? It has not been passed down to 'lower' education. On the contrary, with the growth of knowledge many studies in higher education consist entirely of inert facts unquestioningly asserted, noted, memorized, regurgitated, ticked and graded. Regretfully this is most common in the very sciences and engineering I wish to encourage. The spirit of inquiry must be fostered by creating systems of teaching, and most of all of systems of assessment, that reward it. At the moment researchers in higher education do not teach their research findings and methods sufficiently beyond the circle of other researchers. We leave too much to the journalists, 'Tomorrow's World' and David Attenborough.

With this passionate plea for the growing importance of continuing education you might expect me to advance the argument of increased leisure time. I won't, because I don't believe it. While I accept that working hours have steadily reduced since the Health and Morals Act 1802, the Cotton Mill Acts of 1819 and what *1066 and All That* calls 'the Factory Acts, SatisfacTory Acts and UnsatisfacTory Acts', I do not think this will continue for ever. To my observation our human aspirations increase far more rapidly than our capacity to satisfy them. That satisfaction requires work, so I think there will always be a lot to do. Furthermore, as we know from times of unemployment, people do not like too much leisure. All play and no work leaves Jack unfulfilled. However, I do think leisure will be more important in the future, but not because we will spend more time at it. I think it will be important because there will be increasing social and psychological pressures in the future, and leisure activities must provide one outlet for them.

A New Pattern for Post-Secondary Education (see Fig 2.1)
The need for continuing education means that courses in post-secondary education should be accessible to adults of all ages. Access should be based on maximizing the benefit to the community. In this principle I assume that the students themselves will be major potential beneficiaries according to their ability, experience and motivation. It should be possible to integrate academic and vocational courses at the post-sixteen level. For this reason courses should run for three years, and for many school-leavers this will mean from the age of sixteen to nineteen. Thus entrants to higher education in England without any work experience would typically enter at the age of nineteen, not eighteen.

The examinations, if any, at the age of nineteen +, or for entrance to higher education, could be much more directed towards problems of design, decision making, personal relationships or whatever. Increasingly between the ages of sixteen and nineteen the teaching should consist of asking the question 'why?' Answers will tend to move the area of discourse from applied practical problems to the more theoretical problems of academic disciplines. Thus entrants to higher education may have less factual knowledge than those entering now, but would be well on the way to developing those higher mental skills that we claim to value in higher education.

If you change school curricula to suit the needs of those people leaving education at sixteen + and nineteen +, higher education curricula will have to change too. Instead of beginning with lectures dispensing vast quantities of factual information, higher education should continue the process of presenting practical problems and asking 'why?' The scrutiny of these practical problems will lead to theory. This is crucial; so that there is a gradual drift from general to special, from breadth to

10. JAN. 1985

DELIVERY NOTE - *return*

Order no. ⟶   603470

Squires,G.,ed

Innovation through recession   Research into Higher
Education. Proceedings 6

The Society Guildford 1983

for Res
into Higher Education

1 copy.
0-900868-98-8
£9.00

1/4741

40   ACT   BNB,   22.8.84   09-11-84
S   ⟶ Order date

UNIVERSITY OF SUSSEX LIBRARY

FIGURE 2.1 A New Pattern for post-secondary education

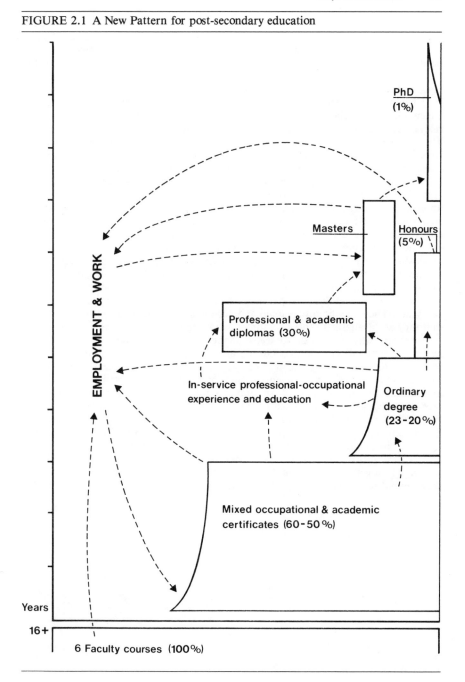

depth, from interdisciplinarity to disciplines, from professional relevance to academic fundamentals and research by asking 'why?' Hence it is an education based upon inquiry and research. Consequently I am not destroying traditional academic departments; indeed I am strengthening their research capacity at a later stage by the earlier development of an inquiring mind, but I want greater departmental co-operation in course teams in the first two years.

I believe that such an approach can reconcile conflicts that have long dogged educational curricula, first by reconciling a liberal education with occupational relevance, and secondly by reconciling the twin demands for breadth and depth. Thirdly, it resolves a problem that has troubled higher education ever since the Renaissance and Descartes: the tension between academic authority and a questioning mind. Academic authority can be sustained so long as the question 'why?' can be answered; thereafter the challenge of doubt is not only legitimate, but credible. I also believe that an education focused upon real problems will teach the application of principles, powers of relevance and the capacity to reason, to criticize, to argue a case and to appreciate another person's point of view. It will give an opportunity to build social and intellectual confidence, even though it cannot ensure that the opportunity will be taken. It may allow the involvement and influence of professional bodies, but without their control. Furthermore, by starting a year later, I believe it goes some way to answering objections to the Pippard proposals for an initial two-year qualification in higher education. However I wish to give much greater emphasis than Pippard to the importance of one-year courses following these two years. They may be professional and vocational or academic; but it is essential that they are available to those wanting continuing and part-time education.

In short, why do I wish to see a change in post-secondary education? The answer lies in the shortcomings of our present system: its over emphasis upon learning facts, its lack of occupational relevance, its social divisiveness, its relative inaccessibility to mature students, the consequent non-contribution of their experience, the narrowness of traditional culture in spite of its claims, the over-specialization in English schools and the non-involvement of the community. Inevitably the changes I propose cannot have been thought through with the same thoroughness as contemporary practice, but they value the art of problem solving, taking responsibility for one's own learning, the wider availability of short courses, greater flexibility in our careers and greater depth for our researchers. These things are brought together by the twin themes of work and the community which I believe are essential to innovation through recession.

3   CONTRACT RESEARCH IN HIGHER EDUCATION

Brian Salter   University of Surrey

There is a widespread belief in higher education that universities, and to a lesser extent polytechnics, are the best places for carrying out research. It is an interesting conceit if only because much of the available evidence suggests the opposite conclusion. Nonetheless it is firmly entrenched and breeds a dangerous over-confidence in higher education's ability to attract research finance, an overconfidence which has so far papered over the expanding gap between the research myth and the research reality. In contrast to this, the view here is that the research system in higher education is currently under severe stress and urgently in need of radical reform. Un-less such reform is rapidly forthcoming the capacity of higher education institutions to obtain research funds and maintain their claim to a major position in the wider research community will be undermined by sheer organizational inefficiency.

Here, the higher education research system is placed in the context of a diverse, and largely unregulated, research funding market. The market is composed of research councils, government departments, industry and private charities and expresses its demand for knowledge (ie research) in different ways. One part of the market may have very specific knowledge demands (eg industry), another may be prepared to negotiate the final form of the demand with the researcher (eg government department) and a third may allow the researcher to define his own demand (eg research councils), though not always. The suppliers of knowledge, in this case the higher education institutions, compete with one another to meet the demand and to obtain research contracts. Other competitors in the same market include industrial research establishments, government in-house research, independent research institutions and quangos. The focus is on the universities, since most of the research in higher education is carried out in the universities and because national data on the public sector's involvement in research is not readily accessible.

THE RESEARCH INFRASTRUCTURE

The recent Merrison Report (1982) on dual funding of university research shows that expenditure on the research infrastructure (equipment, labs, libraries, technicians, etc.) in universities has been declining steadily over the past decade. In political terms, research support has always been regarded as a soft option because, Merrison argues, 'in making economies universities have tended to cut those costs which can most easily and quickly be cut, and these tend to be those related to research' (Merrison, p.3). With the anticipated cuts in the recurrent grant in the order of 11% to 15% between 1979/80 and 1983/84 the prospects for research do not look too bright. Even if the report's recommendations were implemented, Merrison concludes that in the next few years research will be inescapably and substantially damaged (Merrison, p.4) It is worth rehearsing the essentials of Merrison's case, firstly, because unlike previous reports on the dual funding system its statements are for the most part grounded in the best available data and, secondly, because so far few have grasped the full implications of its analysis — least of all the Merrison Committee itself.

Between 1971/72 and 1978/79 there was a 24% growth in the student population from 250,800 to 310,000 while the numbers of teaching staff grew by 13% from 29,400 to 33,300. This meant a worsening of the student/staff ratio from 8.5:1 to 9.3:1 and hence a reduction in that part of the lecturer's time available for pursuing research. Not overwhelmingly serious, perhaps, until one examines the consistent cuts in the research infrastructure which accompanied the expansion of the teaching function of the universities throughout the 1970s. The two types of university activity appear to have been going in opposite directions when seen in terms of the support each received.

In the context of a generally expanding system,[2] the complement of technical and support staff, so vital for sustaining a high quality research effort, *declined* by 6% from 18,400 (1973) to 17,350 (1979). Departmental and laboratory running costs fell from £53.1m in 1971-72 to £43.1m in 1978-79 — a fall of 19% overall but one of 28% when expressed as a reduction per member of staff. Library expenditure increased by 16.7% but, within this, the amount spent on journals (an important part of the research information system) fell by 1%.[3] Most significant of all has been the squeeze on the equipment grant, two-thirds of which it is estimated is spent on research. Here the UGC operates a model of the expenditure deemed necessary and at no point between 1972-73 and 1980-81 has the annual allocation reached the target figure. At present the difference during that period between what should have been spent on equipment and what has been spent stands at £227.9m.

After a decade of attrition, the university research infrastructure is in no state to absorb or withstand the impact of the projected cuts up to 1983-84. Yet there is no reason to suppose that it will not once again be seen as the soft option, the one least likely to arouse opposition. The means by which the block grant is internally distributed varies from university to university and thus the mechanisms for protecting the research base simply do not exist. Furthermore, the problem is bound to persist after 1984, for even if the universities reach the position of level funding the element of committed costs within their budgets will increase as a result of a static academic work force. With no new recruitment of junior staff the rise in the average age and average salary will mean that the committed salary element in the budget must expand at the expense of non-committed costs (eg research support). Unless universities develop a positive science policy, therefore, the steady dismantling of the research base is bound to continue.

THE LABOUR FORCE

At the same time as the research infrastructure is undergoing a rapid decline, the number of contract researchers dependent upon it for their survival is expanding equally rapidly. Between 1972 and 1981 contract researchers increased from 4,985 to 9,688 (a 94% rise), while teaching staff increased from 29,400 to 33,329 (a 13% rise). Looking at it another way, as a proportion of the total academic workforce contract researchers rose from 14% in 1972 to 23% in 1980 and the ratio of teaching to research staff declined from 5.9:1 to 3.4:1 over the same period.[4] Considering these figures, it is difficult to avoid the conclusion that there is a strong negative correlation consistent over time between the numbers of contract researchers and the resources *not* devoted to the research infrastructure. If ever there was a perfectly irrational policy, this is it.

It is paralleled by an equally irrational personnel policy, or non-policy, towards researchers, which has the effect of depriving contract research of a sound professional identity (Figure 3.1). Lacking such an identity, it is inevitable that contract research should be less efficient than it might be. As the demands placed upon the universities by the research funding market have grown, the universities have willingly accepted the money and expanded the labour force but have made little or no attempt to develop a sensible personnel policy for their new employees. They take no responsibility for contract researchers but maximize the political benefits to be gained from contract research money. (Universities are notoriously sensitive to their position in the university research league determined by the proportion of their income which comes from external, ie non-UGC, sources.) The usual term for such an approach is exploitation.

FIGURE 3.1 The cycle of research deprivation

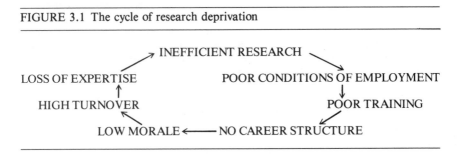

The cycle which reduces the efficiency of university research begins with the conditions of employment for research staff which are, to say the least, primitive. Contracts of employment can vary from a few weeks to, exceptionally, five years, and universities operate them with the bare minimum of employment rights under the law. There is no minimum contract and no period of notice of non-renewal. Researchers are generally obliged to sign away their rights to redundancy pay and protection against unfair dismissal as a condition of employment. Other frequent omissions in the conditions of service include the refusal by universities to provide removal expenses or paid maternity leave.

Nor is the constitutional position of research staff likely to offset their employment marginality and make them feel wanted. University administrative frameworks are organized around UGC-financed personnel and either do not take account of, or specifically exclude, individuals funded on external contracts. In formal constitutional terms, researchers are frequently not members of the decision-making bodies of the institution which employs them. This position is reflected in the absence of rights to vote or stand for office in departmental, faculty or senate elections; utilize faculty conference or research funds; be the 'principal investigator' of a project (ie the named director so far as the funding agency is concerned). The absence of this latter right is obviously of critical importance to a contract researcher wishing to enter the funding market on his own behalf since it means that he is thereby dependent for his survival upon the patronage of a permanent member of the teaching staff.

The training of research staff is very much a hit and miss affair. Theoretically it is the responsibility of the research councils as part of their contribution to the dual funding system. However, as the Swinnerton-Dyer report on postgraduate education makes clear, there is considerable room for improvement and both the SERC and SSRC are taking steps to achieve this. It is noticeable how the report favours the linking of postgraduate and contract research — a sensible arrangement from the viewpoint of the latter since three isolated years on a PhD is probably exactly the wrong preparation for the demands and pressures of contract research and its increasing dependence on teamwork. The move from postgraduate to contract research is not necessarily an easy one.

Institutional marginality coupled with inadequate training for the job provide the initial impetus for the cycle of research deprivation. The absence of a career structure cements the process. As Table 3.1 shows, there really is nowhere for a contract researcher to go in career terms. Almost no researchers (2%) reach the reader, senior lecturer or professional levels and 35% are on the IB grade which as a result of national salary agreements is not available for the employment of teaching staff. Up to the early 1970s, it could be argued that contract research formed an apprenticeship for entry as a lecturer into acadaemia proper and was best seen as part of the teaching career structure. Apart from the fact that this notion was never systematically or consciously applied and served as a convenient rationalization for a pool of cheap research labour, it is no longer supportable. The heady expansionist days of the mid and late 1960s have been replaced by progressive retrenchment in the number of extra teaching jobs available in the seventies culminating in the cuts of the 1980s. Any career mobility between full-time research and teaching is now out of the question. The barriers are up and, like it or not, contract research is on its own.

TABLE 3.1 Salary grading of contract research staff 1980

Grade	Teaching equivalent	N	%
IB		3314	35
IA }	Lecturer	5057	54
II }		823	9
III	Reader/SL	196	2
IV	Professor	43	0
TOTAL		9433	100

SOURCE Universities Statistical Record

Whichever way you look at it, the incentives for an individual remaining part of the labour force on which university research depends are not great. So it is not surprising that poor conditions of employment, low institutional status and the absence of a career structure produce low morale and high turnover of staff. You do not have to be a perfectly rational being to get the market's message. The result is a relatively young and inexperienced workforce (Tables 3.2 and 3.3).

With high turnover of staff, whatever core of research expertise has been established is soon dissipated. Thus any earlier success in the training of researchers is negated by this subsequent stage in the cycle of research deprivation. Equally, it can be fairly stated that the present usage of the university research labour force will produce minimum returns on the investment in its training. There can be few better examples of a waste of training resources.

The cumulative effect of the research deprivation cycle is inefficient research. In her empirical study of the organization of social science research, Jennifer Platt has charted many types of inefficiencies. She lists ill-defined roles, poor managerial skills, ambiguous authority structures, non-existent grievance procedures and examples of all the social consequences which naturally flow from these problems: disagreements, confusions, misunderstandings and, all too often, project fragmentation (Platt 1976). Large-scale knowledge production has organizational requirements which at present are not being met by the poorly trained researcher led by the untrained manager/director. The inefficiences are manifested in terms such as failure to identify funding agency need properly, unrealistic project costing, unmet deadlines, and poor quality reports.

TABLE 3.2 Age of contract research staff 1980

Age	N	%
Under 26	2849	30
27 – 32	3862	41
33 – 38	1586	17
39 – 44	569	6
45 – 50	288	3
50+	279	3
TOTAL	9433	100

SOURCE Universities Statistical Record

TABLE 3.3 Length of service of contract research staff 1980

Years of service	N	%
1 – 5	7684	81
6 – 10	1167	12
11 – 14	335	4
15 – 20	179	2
20+	68	1
TOTAL	9433	100

SOURCE Universities Statistical Record

SCIENCE POLICY AND THE FUNDING MARKET

Although the universities have, as Merrison shows, maintained their position in the funding market over the past decade, it is arguable that they should have tried to improve that position by a more vigorous exploitation of the market while their research infrastructure was still reasonably intact. Now they may be forced into a more competitive stance towards the market whilst lacking the structures to support it. The dual funding system of research is slowly dying of anaemia as the UGC and the universities direct funds away from the research base, and the research councils lack the means, and probably the will, to offset the effects of these trends. In this situation, the only option open to universities, as Merrison observes, is 'to direct their energies and skills more and more towards *attracting externally commissioned research*' (Merrison, p.25, my stress) — always assuming they want to maintain a research capacity. One very good reason for doing so is that otherwise they are likely to lose out according to one criterion for the allocation of the recurrent grant. Quoting Merrison again:

> 'While it would be wrong, therefore, for the totality of UGC research support to be determined in relation to the level of external grants, it would be right to recognize that external grant income is an important factor which should be taken into account, alongside a range of others.' (Merrison, p.30)

What are the prospects for the universities improving their position in the research funding market and what policies would assist their efforts? Their present position is summarized in Table 3.4.

TABLE 3.4 Total grants and contracts for university scientific research 1971/72 and 1978/79

	£m (1978/79 prices)	
	1971/72	1978/79
Research councils	56	54
Government departments	10	14
Charitable trusts and foundations } The Royal Society }	13	15
Other income	25	40
TOTAL	104	123

SOURCE Merrison Report Appendix P

On their own these figures appear reasonably optimistic since they show that the universities have increased the amount they obtain from the funding market by 18% (£19m) between 1971/72 and 1978/79. However, an examination of their share of each sub-sector of the market produces different conclusions. Of the research councils' total income of £331.6m in 1978/79, only £204.53 (62%) went in support of university research, of which £54m consisted of grants and contracts. In addition, while the research councils' total income *rose* by 8% between 1971/72 and 1978/79 (£306.2m to £331.6m) the amount allocated to grants and contracts *declined* by 3½% (£56m to £54m).[5] So the universities have marginally suffered in an area of the market in which they supposedly have a monopoly. In the charities sector, the figures are not comprehensive enough for a general statement but in the case of medical charities universities have retained about 36% of the available research funds over the past decade.[6]

Where the universities are making very few inroads is in the government research and development sector. Here their share is £14m out of a total of £1,346m — ie 1%;[7]

a figure which the Merrison Report, with cautious understatement, describes as 'surprisingly small' and 'a real cause for concern' (Merrison, p.21). The 'Other Income' category must remain an enigma because information is not available to indicate how far it consists of funds from industry for example. The lack of data is unfortunate because it is the 60% growth in this category over the last decade which almost entirely accounts for the growth in university research income.

Universities' competitiveness in the funding market is dependent upon four main factors. They have a monopoly of certain knowledge areas, they are high status institutions, they carry out some high quality research (albeit inefficiently) and they do it comparatively cheaply. The problem they are likely to face in the near future is that a change in the fourth factor, the cost of research, may encourage funding agencies to re-evaluate the other three. Up to now, the UGC has effectively subsidized externally financed research projects in universities. In the case of research council research this is a legitimate part of the dual funding system. However, other externally funded research is supposed to cover the full cost of its use of university facilities, has rarely done so and has relied on the UGC block grant to absorb the resulting deficit. But with the reductions in the UGC monies, contract research is coming under increasing pressure from universities to cost itself realistically.

If, as a result, funding agencies find that university-based research is becoming more expensive they will almost certainly question the extent to which they are getting value for money. And if the answer is not at all obvious because universities are not used to having to justify themselves to outsiders then the attraction of knowledge monopoly, high status and occasional high quality research may fade somewhat in the eyes of funding agencies. This does not necessarily mean that funders will withdraw support from the university sector altogether but it does imply that they will develop more rigorous criteria for scrutinizing research applications. Those universities which can readily demonstrate that they have developed, or are developing, a policy for the training and retention of skilled research personnel will obviously be better placed to argue that they can supply value for money in the form of high quality, efficient research. In short, they will be more competitive.

If the university system is to obtain a larger share of the research funding market it will need to develop a science policy which harnesses and rationalizes the resources at its disposal. Difficult choices will have to be made both by the UGC and by individual institutions regarding the maintenance of the research infrastructure. It will have to be accepted that the dual funding system has already withered on the vine — something which the Merrison Report, in a supreme exercise of doublethink, both clearly demonstrates in its analysis and refuses to acknowledge in its conclusions.

Given that it is not possible, if it ever was, to maintain a research 'floor' for all universities, how is the UGC to identify which institutions should receive research support? Merely relying on the proportion of a university's income which comes from external research sources is too gross a measure. It obscures the strengths and weaknesses, as well as the potential that institutions have in particular fields regardless of the overall level of external funds. If the UGC is to allocate its research support sensibly, therefore, it will need more information from individual institutions. Universities will have to establish mechanisms which can prioritize areas of research activity (Merrison recommends 'Research Committees'). In particular research fields it may make sense for groups of institutions to establish regional consortia.

It is clearly desirable for the UGC to collaborate with the research councils in this exercise since it would be unfortunate if the siting of research bases (UGC funded) and research training and projects (research council funded) did not coincide, or at least overlap. Collaboration would also be necessary if the so-called 'new blood' scheme were to be introduced, whereby 800 'bright, young academics' would be given three to five-year fellowships. As it stands the scheme is of little relevance to any strategy designed to improve the universities' ability to attract contract research. It would merely give an added twist to the cycle of research deprivation by introducing a fresh batch of inexperienced researchers on short-term contracts, with few funding networks and hence little capacity to obtain the necessary research finance to help either themselves, or others, to survive. They would merely be a burden on a contract research system which is already bottom heavy with inexperience. The scheme at present is the antithesis of what is needed, given the demands of the funding market.

What is needed to sustain and expand university research is the injection of money to pump prime academics with the ability to conduct and manage contract research and exploit the funding market. As Table 3.2 shows, at present these individuals are being lost as soon as they have learnt their trade. If the 'new blood' schemes were operated in this way it would be an added pressure on universities to establish research committees to make the selection. Properly implemented, the scheme could be an instrument for creating a core of skilled personnel with the ability to give impetus, direction, identity and, hopefully, stability to an expanding contract research activity.

At the same time, consideration also has to be given to a number of supporting moves to break the cycle of research deprivation. First, how is continuity to be given to non-core personnel? It is no good having a core of researchers supported by a constant change of colleagues. One way of tackling this problem is to impose a surcharge on the market for preserving the expertise the market needs. This could take the form, for example, of part of a project's overheads being channelled into a university bridging fund to cover both minimum length contracts and gaps between a researcher's contracts. Secondly, researchers will have to be flexible enough to adapt to changing market demands. That is to say, they will need a base of transferable skills to which can be swiftly added the particular knowledge required to carry out a particular project. On the university side, this means maintaining a reflexive staff development programme for researchers, possibly in conjunction with postgraduate training, so that updating can take place as and when necessary. Regular reviews would be required of available research support resources (eg computing and laboratory facilities). Thirdly, within the terms of their contract, research staff will have to be given due recognition as full members of the university by means of parity of conditions of service and constitutional rights and teaching staff.

Gearing a science policy to the twin goals of breaking the cycle of research deprivation and acquiring a larger share of the research funding market is unlikely to find favour with everyone. By rationalizing the contract research areas of university activity, such a policy would direct away from the broad base funding underpinning the concept that 'every teacher is a researcher'. (Limited resources mean that this is happening anyway but the process would be accelerated and organized.) Individual lecturers would be obliged to take cognizance of university and UGC policy on research before selecting their own research area. Academic freedom would be constrained in so far as some areas of research would be seen to be better supported than others. (Again, this happens already but is not the result of deliberate policy.) Although some may consider such changes to be too high a price to pay, the perpetuation of existing trends holds few attractions. A steadily fragmenting research infrastructure and an increasingly sceptical research funding market cannot be combated with old university myths. New ones are needed.

NOTES
1   The previous reports on the dual funding system are: Council for Scientific Policy *Report of a Study on the Support of Scientific Research in the Universities* Cmnd 4798, October 1971; *First and Second Reports from the Select Committee on Science and Technology on Scientific Research in British Universities* 1974/75 and 1975/76. All the figures in this section are taken from the Merrison Report.
2   University income (recurrent grant plus student fees less charges levied for rates) rose from £718.6m in 1971-72 to £800.7m in 1978-79 — an increase of 11%.
3   In 1981 the Royal Society produced *A Study of the Scientific Information System in the UK* which concluded that the scientific information system was becoming unstable because libraries could not afford to buy expensive journals, and publishers could not afford to publish them unless they did.
4   Figures taken from the Merrison Report, p.8, and the UGC *Annual Survey, 1980-81* Cmnd 8663 (HMSO 1982) p.16.
5   Figures calculated from the Merrison Report, Appendix L.
6   Figures calculated from the Merrison Report, Appendix O.
7   Figures calculated from the Merrison Report, Appendix N.

REFERENCES
Merrison Report. Advisory Board for the Research Councils and the Universities Grants Committee (1982) *Report of a Joint Working Party on the Support of University Scientific Research* Cmnd 8576 HMSO
Platt, J. (1976) *Realities of Social Research* Sussex UP, Chatto and Windus Ltd.

4 THE EDUCATIONAL CONSELLING AND CREDIT TRANSFER INFORMATION SERVICE

Peter Toyne   North East London Polytechnic

In the context of access to higher and further education (HFE), credit transfer is a process whereby qualifications, part-qualifications and learning experiences are given recognition (or credit) to enable students to progress without having to repeat material or levels of study, to transfer from one course to another, and to gain further educational experience and qualifications, thereby contributing to the maximization of accumulated educational capital.

The importance of facilitating the award of credits for previous academic, professional and vocational studies and the transfer of credits between courses and institutions has been increasingly often recognized and in November 1975 the DES wrote to the national bodies principally concerned. The response suggested that there might be value in establishing national arrangements on credit transfers. The then Minister of State called a meeting in July 1977 of representatives of the organizations, and it was decided that a study should be undertaken into the necessity and feasibility of establishing a national information service on credit transfer. A steering committee was set up. It first met in October 1977 and elected as chairman Dr C.C. Butler, Vice-Chancellor of the University of Technology, Loughborough; soon afterwards the feasibility study was established with the following terms of reference:

> 'To advise on the necessity, feasibility and cost of establishing and running a service for recording and providing information on credits which are being given by academic and professional institutions in the United Kingdom, towards Further and Higher Educational qualifications, in respect of previous studies undertaken by students.'

Inquiries were made to establish the present scale and nature of credit transfer; the need for a national information service; and the feasibility of implementing a service capable of matching the demonstrated need. Two major surveys were conducted to assess the needs of possible institutional users of a credit transfer information service, and to assess the extent to which such a service might be used by students who left their courses without completing them. Three special studies were commissioned to examine the particular problems of transfer connected with the DipHE and the HND, to consider the need for transfer information in adult and continuing education, and to assess the potential usefulness of viewdata for a national information service.

THE EXTENT OF CREDIT TRANSFER

The final report (Toyne 1979) was considered and approved by the steering committee in June 1979 and submitted to the Secretary of State for Education. Part I of that report examined the three main ways in which the process of credit transfer was operating in the UK, viz:

a In the recognition of 'alternative' qualifications for initial entry to educational courses.

b   In the granting of exemption from parts of courses (entry with 'advanced standing') to candidates with suitable previous experience.

c   In the introduction and development of study schemes based specifically on the principle of cumulative and transferable credit.

It reported that provision was made for the consideration of alternative qualifications for initial entry to courses in almost all forms of post-secondary education, including the professional institutions, and 'open entry' was characteristic of much of non-advanced FE and the courses offered by the Open University. In almost all cases, applications for admission with alternative qualifications were considered on their individual merits, and where more formal arrangements had been made they were advisory rather than mandatory and each case was still considered individually. It was also reported that the number and proportion of students applying for and being admitted to courses in higher and further education, including those of the professional institutions, through alternative or open entry routeways had appreciably increased during the last decade so that about 15 per cent of applications and 11 per cent of admissions to university first degree courses were of students offering alternative qualifications and between 15 per cent and 20 per cent polytechnic applications and approximately 20 per cent polytechnic admissions were estimated to be in this category. The proportion of applications and enrolments in this category on college and professional institution courses was estimated to be approximately 25 per cent.

The practice of granting advanced standing in HFE for students with qualifications or part-qualifications was found not to be widespread in the UK, though in recent years it had become less unusual as specific provision for it had been built into several different study schemes. Formal agreements had also been concluded between the Open University and the CNAA, and between the Open University and a number of other universities, which enabled this 'advanced standing' to be accorded, in appropriate cases, to students wishing to transfer between those institutions. However, a major concern in admitting students with advanced standing remained that of ensuring a realistic and appropriate 'match' between previous courses and those for which admission was being sought, so that students were not disadvantaged.

It was estimated that approximately 6 per cent of university and polytechnic admissions in 1977-78 were with advanced standing, and that over a half of all registered Open University students had also gained entry with advanced standing. Almost 40 per cent of applications for student membership of the professional award-making bodies were found to have included requests for advanced standing.

Study schemes involving modular structures and cumulative and transferable credits were found to be quite familiar in the UK. Two national schemes (the Open University and the awards of the Technician Education Council (TEC)) incorporated a high degree of flexibility which enabled students to accumulate credits and to transfer as necessary, and it was estimated that during the 1978-79 session some 130,000 students were enrolled on courses in these two systems. The Business Education Council (BEC) scheme also operated at national level and was similarly modular in nature; it involved the accumulation of credit and had provision for transferability. Some 80,000 students were actually enrolled on its courses during the 1978-79 session. The remaining schemes either were local or were internal to individual institutions.

It was concluded that a very wide variety of different educational opportunities in higher and further education existed in the UK and that there was an increasingly wide variety in the number of qualificational and experiential routeways by which access to those opportunities could be secured. Practices, however, were found to vary between institutions in terms of their entry requirements and their attitudes to alternative qualifications and transfer with advanced standing, so that intending students found it very hard to discover precisely what opportunities were really available.

A NATIONAL INFORMATION SERVICE

The need for a national information service which could publicize the available opportunities was analysed in Part 2 of the report. Four sets of needs were examined:

a   The needs of the educational and professional institutions.
b   The needs of potential students and their advisers and those who provide information for them.
c   The needs of the national award-making bodies and the existing information and advisory services.
d   The needs which may arise from anticipated, proposed and current changes in course structures, curriculum development and syllabus content, and in the organization of professional, continuing, higher and further education, together with the development of EEC requirements to encourage European transfers.

The views of the main award-making professional institutions and establishments of HFE on these matters were sought by questionnaire and visits. In all, 821 establishments and professional bodies were contacted and 586 usable returns were received. The main difficulties they experienced in obtaining information on which to assess applications for advanced standing or for entry with alternative qualifications were said to be in finding existing information. The search process was claimed to be time-consuming: information of different kinds being available in several different places; furthermore, it was said that such information was not always of the right kind, or in a suitable form. A common observation was that access to improved information through a central service would be helpful, and there was agreement that any new service should be capable not only of providing information quickly at the request of individual institutions but also of circulating all institutions with information on newly-concluded agreements affecting entry qualifications and credit transfer generally. In short, it was evident that existing information sources in the UK were generally considered to be inadequate, or in need of improvement.

It was estimated that any new service needed to be capable of dealing with not less than 18,000 inquiries per year from the estimated 600 institutions likely to use it. There was a pattern of demand-peaking in the inquiries made of existing services, such peaking coinciding with the main period in which applications are made to the institutions (the autumn in the case of university applications, and mid to late summer for most others). It was recommended therefore, that any new service should be capable of dealing with a similar pattern of demand-peaking.

Clearly a new service for institutional users would indirectly benefit potential students through facilitating the decision-making processes in admitting institutions. But it was shown in the surveys that potential students also had a more direct need for a service enabling them to discover what opportunities there were for credit transfer and what different qualifications were recognized. General information was available, in part, in different publications, but it was not easy for students to obtain details or advice, as was revealed in the survey of those who left courses without completing them. As many as 45.5 per cent of the respondents were not in possession of information which might have assisted them to transfer to another course. Instead they discontinued their education.

Opinion was divided on the extent to which, the way in which and the form in which information might or should be made available to students and those who advise them. One reservation concerned the possible publication of past admission decisions and any precedent which might easily, yet erroneously, be implied from such listings. Institutions were concerned about the confidentiality of the listings and it was clear that any national information service would need to ensure the anonymity of its information.

The views of most other organizations involved in making national educational awards and/or in providing educational information was that a national information service on credit transfer would be both supported and used by many of them. The Open University and the CNAA had already endorsed a mutual general policy paper by the time the feasibility study was set up, the substance of which was to recommend the establishment of a transfer agency between the two of them.

It was also the view of the City and Guilds of London Institute (CGLI), BEC, and TEC that a national information service on credit transfer would be desirable, and most organizations suggested that a national information service could also potentially assist and draw upon the work of most of the existing information providers.

Account was also taken of possible changes in the present organization and form of HFE; a common view was that the future HFE system would seem likely to include provision for greater flexibility in educational access and modes of study. These would necessitate a close examination of many aspects of the present system, including teaching methods, accommodation, residential patterns, timetabling and awards systems. It was suggested that if a more 'open-ended' model of this kind were developed, admission and selection procedures would need to provide for the assessment of many different 'alternative' qualifications, including experiential learning, and for greater provision for advanced standing. Similarly, several observers maintained that study schemes would need to be increasingly formulated in terms of transferable and cumulative credits, which might contribute to the development of a more flexible system. On both counts, therefore, there would be a manifest need to establish a national information service to assist students and institutions in matters relating to credit transfer.

Reservations were expressed about the way in which the new information service could create an undesirable and excessive bureaucracy, and the possibility that it could lead to the institutionalization of practices and to the creation, rather than the diminution, of barriers to educational access. The need for it to remain advisory, and in no way to encroach upon the autonomy of individual institutions was repeatedly stressed. The evidence indicated, however, that provided these reservations were taken into account, a national information service on credit transfer would provide both institutional and student users with a facility for which there was a clear need.

THE FEASIBILITY OF THE SERVICE
The third part of the report went on to consider the actual feasibility of establishing such a service, and concluded that, in general, it would indeed be possible to obtain sufficient information of the right kind on which to base a service matching most of

the needs of institutional and student users, but it would take time to build it up. It was shown that the new service would be able to draw upon and collate existing data and experience, but that such data were not generally available at present. In this way it would create a new and central data bank both from its own and from existing sources.

The amount of information to be held would clearly be considerable and would relate to a large number and variety of qualifications (estimated to be about 5,000 initially) at different educational levels both in the UK and overseas. Four main categories of information were identified and related to descriptions of courses and qualifications, institutional practices in accepting alternative qualifications for initial entry or in granting advanced standing, recommendations and agreements on qualifications and the progress or achievement obtained by credit transfer students.

It was apparent at once that it would be necessary to store much of the information in 'free-form' (ie without unnecessary abbreviation), though under a number of codified headings. It would also be necessary to be able to retrieve the information flexibly in order to suit different user-requirements and, in particular, in order to produce aggregated, abbreviated or abstracted information. Ease of access would be of paramount importance. If the service were to be effective for institutional users, it would be necessary to retrieve information quickly.

These different requirements presented problems since they were in some ways self-conflicting. On the one hand, the quantity and security of the information involved, together with the need for flexibility of its retrieval, were such that the facilities afforded by computer storage and retrieval systems would be required; on the other hand, whilst it was possible to envisage a large mainframe computer system designed to handle the volume of information involved and capable of direct interrogation by users, the cost of installing and operating such a system would be prohibitive.

There were also differences in the form of access required which were difficult to reconcile with the need for speed and security and the need to provide tailor-made free-form replies. A computer-based system could be designed to provide security and on-line access for those who needed it, but it would not be able to provide tailor-made hard copies of the requested (free-form) information without incurring high costs.

A solution was suggested in the development of a hybrid information storage and retrieval system. By using a word-processing system and a real-time data-based management (mini) computer system, together with a manual library, it appeared possible to design a workable, flexible and cost-effective system which could be implemented quickly and easily, using a non-specialist staff. All available published material would be collected and held in an indexed library, qualification descriptions would be abstracted manually as required and transferred to a flexible diskette for subsequent recall through the word-processing system. Individualized free-form hard-copy replies could thus be easily obtained from an ever-increasing bank of basic descriptive information relating to the most frequently requested courses or qualifications.

Information on institutional practices, recommendations and agreements, and on student progress and achievement, for which greater security and flexibility were required, would, however, be held on a real-time computer system. Such information as was required from this source in reply to a specific inquiry could be easily incorporated into whatever other descriptive material might be needed from the word-processing system, in order to produce a single reply containing information from both sources.

Other essential facilities which it was suggested the computer system could provide included the cataloguing of the library of publications, and the identification and provision of information on those qualifications which might be suitable for inclusion in publications it may be necessary to produce. With the development of such publications and the use of viewdata to disseminate very basic information about the facilities available, it seemed possible to record and provide information in a way which would meet most of the different user-requirements.

The surveys in Part 2 of the report had clearly shown that any service providing information about transfers would need to be seen as a body independent of any one sector, organization, institution or interest — whether in HFE or in the commercial and industrial world. Equally, it was clear that the success of the service would be dependent upon the continued goodwill, support and guidance of all concerned with post-secondary education in the UK. Yet there appeared to be no existing organization which could be asked to assume responsibility for the proposed new service, granted that it was vital for it to be seen as independent and with a separate management structure allowing for the broad representation of several different organizations.

Neither did any existing organizations have the spare physical capacity (4500 sq.ft) which would be needed for a national information service and which would enable scale economies to be achieved through the shared use of their accommodation and other administrative or technical facilities. The more realistic suggestion was thus to establish a new body (managed by an executive council advised by a general steering committee) in the form of a non-profit-making private company limited by guarantee and registered as a charitable organization. A two-year pilot scheme would be needed to prepare the basic information and the detailing of the service's day-to-day operations and organization before any service could be made available. Even then, it was pointed out that it would be operationally impossible for the new service to introduce all of the required facilities simultaneously to all potential users.

The report concludes that it would be in the interests of potential students if the service were initially to concentrate on providing a service for institutional users, including the professional bodies. This would enable the quantity, quality and usefulness of the data bank to be built up more rapidly, and facilitate the consideration of credit transfer requests by the institutions themselves. Since a service for institutions was shown to command more support than a direct service for students, such a phasing would allow further time to be devoted to devising an effective direct service for students. It was thus recommended that a service should be made available to all potential users as soon as was practicable.

The cost of the initial setting-up exercise was estimated at £190,000 per annum, while the operational service for institutional users was estimated at approximately £220,000 per annum and a service including student users estimated at £260,000 per annum. Although it was possible to envisage a largely self-financing scheme, the report recommended that central direct financing would be essential for at least the setting-up operation and a period of time beyond that (about three years, but dependent upon the phasing-in of the student service). It further suggested that if charges were then to be introduced, a small grant would probably be necessary to cover any shortfall in charge revenue and any cost of services and operations for which a charge could not be made. On balance, however, it was recommended that user-charges should only be introduced once the service was fully established. It would then be possible for the scheme to be essentially, though not entirely, self-financing.

In summary then, the project team concluded that it would be feasible to establish a national information service capable of recording and providing information on credit transfer possibilities. An initial period of approximately two years would be needed for the acquisition and preparation of the basic information and the detailing of the service's day-to-day operations and organization before it could be offered first to institutional users and later to potential student users.

Central financing would need to be sought for a period of up to approximately five years. Thereafter, user-charges might be introduced in order to make the scheme largely self-financing. The service would need to be independent of any existing institutions, organizations or sectors of HFE. A new body should be established in the form of a non-profit-making private company limited by guarantee and registered as a charitable organization which would be responsible for the management and development of the service.

This service would help to meet the need of many in HFE and would have a significant effect in avoiding unnecessary duplication of resources generally, in saving on resources in individual institutions, in promoting greater awareness of the available opportunities for credit transfer and thus in reducing the current high wastage in individual effort.

FURTHER SURVEYS
There then followed (in 1980) a series of more detailed surveys of the information likely to be required by students and educational advisers using the new service. Of 220 advisory services consulted (university, polytechnic, local authority and adult careers and guidance services), 172 replied, from which it was estimated that they would make some 50,000 inquiries a year of an effective information service. The bulk of these inquiries (about 90 per cent) would come from LEA advisory services in respect of students at further education colleges. The Council of Local Education Authorities considered that it would be reasonable to charge for the use of the service.

The student survey produced 9,917 replies (about 60 per cent response, of which 2,116 were from students over the age of 25). About 95 per cent of these students considered that the service would be useful or very useful and the majority thought it reasonable to pay about £3 or £4 for it. Even if interpreted conservatively, this evidence suggested that a substantial number of educational and professional institutions, the bulk of student advisory services and a great many individual higher and further education students would use the service even if charges were levied. The demand likely to arise from adult and continuing education was not specifically tested but research by specialist bodies in this increasingly important field suggested that the service could have a vital part to play, particularly for mature students entering or re-entering higher education and for those seeking post-experience vocational courses for retraining or updating their knowledge.

It also became clearer that there was a strong feeling among students and their advisers that the information service should be linked closely to educational counselling services — an observation which finally led to the conclusion that the new service should be developed as an educational counselling and credit transfer information service (ECCTIS).

At the same time, more detailed research was conducted into the computer requirements for the proposed service. However, this was only a provisional, outline assessment and because of the increased demand and new orientation indicated by the student surveys, the DES next asked the Open University to review the operational requirements for ECCTIS, consider the alternative computer systems and provide estimates of the order of magnitude of costs.

DEVELOPMENTS AND IMPLICATIONS

In the light of this advice ministers concluded that while the studies so far undertaken were encouraging with regard to the potential demand for and feasibility of ECCTIS, as well as the willingness of users to pay for it, there were many outstanding questions which could only be resolved by an operational trial. Only a trial could test the systems to be devised and the enthusiasm of institutions and others to participate. They accordingly authorized a pilot operation in the area of the South Western Regional Advisory Council. It is expected that the Centre to be established will have information on all courses of further and higher education leading to recognized qualifications (except school-leaving examinations) in all further education institutions in that region, with in addition those of all United Kingdom universities and of polytechnics in England and Wales. It will be open to inquiries from students' advisers in the region and to institutional inquiries from anywhere in the United Kingdom.

When the new service was announced, a considerable interest was shown in the educational press and elsewhere, with the protagonists of credit transfer claiming that the proposals did not go far enough and the antagonists proclaiming that 'the American academic cafeteria is here' and that 'it will be the end of the British system of HE as we know it'. The time is therefore right to consider carefully what the practical implications of credit transfer are for such time-honoured features of our system as the length, phasing, mode and location of study in higher education; more significantly, however, it is important to recognize the implications of credit transfer systems for the very *nature* and *content* of academic programmes. In short, credit transfer fundamentally challenges our hitherto almost unswerving devotion to the development of three-year, full-time, 'holistic' degree programmes studied in one institution immediately at the end of full-time school studies, and leads us to ask three major questions.

First, is the full-time three-year degree programme for eighteen-year-olds likely to be the most desirable offering in the HE system of the 1980s and beyond? Why should it be three years? Are there better alternatives, eg $2 + 2$ or credit-rated modules/units collected flexibly over a longer (finite?) period of time including part-time study? Why should there be only one programme and formulated primarily for 18-year-olds?

Secondly, should degree (and sub-degree) programmes (of whatever length) continue to be designed in such a way that learning experiences tend to be confined to relatively narrow specialisms (as now) or would it be educationally and socially more desirable to have more *general* topics (and credit for work experience) specifically built in to such programmes (in a typical scheme based on credit transfer modules, students might be required to 'pick and mix' their credits in order to achieve a better balance between specialism and generalism). What topics would be regarded as useful additions/alternatives if such a scheme were adopted?

Thirdly, should students necessarily expect to complete their HE study programmes in *one* institution? The mutual recognition of appropriate credits potentially frees educational provision from a single locational tie — as such it could be the means by which 'centres of excellence' in particular fields could contribute more effectively to a national pattern of subject provision in different institutions. Furthermore, the educational experience for students to be gained from moving between different institutions could be considerable (even if it produced bureaucratic problems in recording and transcribing credits obtained).

If the answers to these three questions are essentially 'Yes', there is little need any further to consider the development of credit transfer in our system of awards. On the other hand, if the answers to these questions are essentially 'No', the development of credit transfer as a central feature of the awards systems in HE would undoubtedly enable the present somewhat monolithic system to be changed to make it possibly more attractive to students and employers, through the more flexible study schemes which it could promote. A whole sequence of interlocking awards could be designed from sub-degree to higher degree level, in which full credit (or recognition) for earlier work could be taken into account, and into which different kinds of learning experiences, gained sequentially in different places and more flexibly at different periods of time, could be more fully incorporated than at present. It is said by some that the advent of ECCTIS is but the tip of a large and potentially damaging educational iceberg which is now floating in the sea of academic awards. What, however, could be damaging about it, if it caused us to re-think very carefully the present highly traditional system and if, in turn, it caused us to propose a more exciting and logical system designed to meet future, rather than past, needs?

REFERENCE
Toyne, P. (1979) *Education Credit Transfer: Feasibility Study* London: DES

5 STRUCTURAL BARRIERS TO INNOVATION IN WEST GERMANY

Friedemann Schmithals   *University of Bielefeld*

The present economic recession affects West German and English educational institutions in roughly the same way. However, it is not only the extent of the cuts imposed on higher education that determines the chances for innovation under the present economic conditions. The institutions are equally strongly influenced by the traditions of their respective educational systems, their legal basis and their real standing in the life of a society. The fundamental differences between the English and the German educational systems have always invited comparisons. Comparing the different systems and their traditions promises to provide valuable information about the adequacy of the developments planned in each country.

This is also true of the present restrictive conditions under which a comparison of the two systems should point towards potential developments in one or other of them. In that sense I would like to draw attention to a few aspects of the German system which seem to me to be important in connection with the capacity for innovation within higher education. My central point is this: the important and still pervasive traditions of the German educational system make it increasingly difficult under conditions of dwindling resources to find solutions which, from a pedagogical and scientific point of view, are the most responsible ones possible.

This thesis does not of course mean that there has not been or will not be any change in the system of higher education. This system is in fact developing quite rapidly. But in which areas and to what ends? I am conscious of the fact that the acceptability of my assertion strongly depends on whether or not my idea of what substantial reforms are is accepted.

THE HISTORICAL DEVELOPMENT OF GERMAN HIGHER EDUCATION

State activities in higher education have a long tradition in Germany. A telling token of this may be the fact that without exception all the older universities founded before 1900 within what is now the Federal Republic and still in existence today bear the name of a former monarch. However, it must be borne in mind that the old German 'Reich' was a more or less loose confederation of independent kingdoms, principalities and dukedoms, and that the universities were institutions of the single states. Down to the end of the eighteenth century, the universities were institutions directly dependent on the ruler of the individual state. Their main function was to educate future servants for both state and church. It was the state which directly appointed the professional staff and which supervised the observance of the law in their teaching. In keeping with medieval economic principles, the universities and/or the individual professors usually derived their income from endowments bestowed on them by the state. Only in so far as this meant that there was no direct financing by the state was it possible to talk of any independence among the universities at all.

The early nineteenth century was the period of comprehensive university reform. At first Napoleon's rule led to the disappearance of about half of the numerous universities of the time. Meanwhile, however, the lively development of the arts and sciences was felt to be an important element in intellectual and political revival.

The outstanding event in this revival was the foundation of the University of Berlin in 1810 at a time of extreme political weakness in the Prussian state. Here, the final breach with the scholastic tradition of administering and handing down knowledge was put into effect; instead, the emphasis was now on the creative productivity of the intellect. Consequently, administrative limitations on research and teaching were lifted. The university was autonomous in all its internal affairs. At the same time, however, the university was becoming fully integrated into the budget of the state; the professors became civil servants and were given special rights. The foundation of the University of Berlin proved to be particularly successful and led to a rapid development of scientific life. Due to Prussia's dominance in the Germany after Napoleon, the constitution of Berlin's university became a model for the reform of all other universities. For the overwhelming majority of students (lawyers, teachers, doctors) studies finished with a state examination. Passing this examination was the prerequisite for but also to a large extent the guarantee of employment by the state. Admission to university was granted to anyone who had successfully passed the final examination of a state 'Gymnasium' (grammar school). Other roads of access to university no longer existed.

The constitution of higher education as it evolved at the beginning of the nineteenth century under Prussian leadership is in important parts still in force today. The republican constitutions of 1919 and 1949 gave the principle of the freedom of academic research and instruction the character of a basic right. When, in 1871, the Prussian-German empire was proclaimed, all cultural affairs remained within the exclusive responsibility of the individual states. There have been no fundamental changes in that respect either: the old regional states have been replaced by the states (Länder) of the Federal Republic of Germany.

When, in the nineteenth century, German science attained a leading position in many areas, there was a considerable rise in the evaluation and esteem in which the universities, the sciences and scientists were held. A university professor appeared as a person whose personal achievement, rather than protection or hereditary prerogatives, had secured him the highest position that science could offer. In his person, all privileges granted to the university were concentrated. In his department he was the absolute ruler; together with his colleagues he decided the fate of the university. The university developed into a 'scholars republic'. But in this republic it was exclusively the professors who were free.

The traditions pinpointed in this rough sketch can all be seen to have left traces in West German higher education today:

— Institutions in higher education are state institutions; staff are civil servants or state employees. However, there is no central control: every land is (in principle) completely independent in its decisions on matters of higher education in its own sphere.
— The constitution guarantees the basic right of the principle of the freedom of research and instruction.
— Within higher education professors constitute a group with special privileges.
— The institutions of higher education are exclusively scientific institutions.

CONSEQUENCES FOR INNOVATION

I will now try to sketch out what is implied in the situation described above for the practicability of reforms. The central role of science and technology in modern civilization, the development of huge universities and the considerable cost of the education system have all increased the pressure for more public planning of education in all countries, including those with traditions of little state activity in the educational field. In this, a centrally administered education system offers the prospect of rational central planning and the consistent enforcement of fundamental educational policies. There is, however, the danger of limited flexibility and inappropriate uniformity. On the other hand, a system without strong central guidance can be expected to be flexible in terms of individual demands, though possibly rather cumbersome in terms of the implementation of fundamental educational policies. Does the system within the Federal Republic, which in some respect occupies an intermediate position between these two extremes, lead to a summation of the advantages or of the disadvantages? In other words, what chance does the federal but at the same time centralized system of higher education in the Federal Republic offer in attempts to reform higher education?

There are essentially two instruments used in the Federal Republic to co-ordinate educational planning at the federal level. On the one hand, the federal government and parliament can define certain basic principles through a legal framework binding for all individual states, without formally interfering with their sovereignty. Measures along these lines, though, are dependent on previous agreement by all federal states. In addition to that, the states themselves have created a 'Konferenz der Kulturminister' (KMK), ie a standing conference of their education secretaries, to co-ordinate their educational policies. Important measures in higher education are discussed and co-ordinated by the respective ministries of the individual states, within the framework of this conference. In areas where there is basically a common interest of the various states, these instruments have proved to be sufficient to ensure the necessary degree of co-ordination. In the past, basic questions as to the extension of higher education, and indeed all quantitative aspects of policy, have been agreed on in this way with relatively few conflicts. These areas are therefore characterized by an essentially centralized administration. On the other hand, questions of instruction and learning, ie whatever pertains to the content and methods of instruction, depend to a much higher degree on competing influences of a philosophical and/or (party) political nature. In these areas the constant need to find a political consensus tends to lead to compromise solutions which can be explained as the result of haggling between the parties but which often make little sense as a solution to the problem at hand. For instance, the close connection between final examination and career means that again and again questions connected with these examinations have found a centralized and administrative solution. In this way, the scope of the individual institution to influence examinations is severely restricted. In addition, since obviously there is a very close connection between the examination system and the study programme, this set-up has an immediate influence on the form and content of instruction and learning. Thus the federal system does not — as might have been expected — lead to 'bold experiments' nor does it lead to a multiplicity of educational opportunities. On the contrary, the tendency is towards greater uniformity on the basis of the lowest common denominator of political compromises. The individual states (or groups of states) obstruct each others' reform programmes and in doing so restrict the scope of the individual institution as well.

The problem of administrative obstacles to innovatory experiments resulting from this state of affairs have been known for a long time. That is why, at the beginning of the 1970s, opportunities were created to concede and to finance reforms in university teaching outside existing norms, in so-called pilot experiments. The responsibility for this lies with the 'Bund-Länder-Kommission für Bildungsplanung und Forschungsförderung', a joint body of federal and state representatives concerned with educational planning and research promotion founded in 1970. Between 1970 and 1980 a great number of experiments in the field of university teaching have been supported by it. However, suffering the usual fate of such pilot experiments, it has ended in a comprehensive report without establishing permanent changes.

The most ambitious project of this kind (albeit with a somewhat different legal basis) has been an attempt to change the education of lawyers. For about ten years, at ten of the newly-founded universities, lawyers have been educated following curricula essentially aimed at a greater integration of practical demands with academic studies. All of the universities concerned have invested and are still investing a lot of time and money in evaluating the new curricula. The experimental phase is due to come to an end soon and a decision must be taken as to which approach to the education of lawyers is going to be the compulsory one in future. Major party political controversies have already developed around the question and it would be surprising if any of the insights gained during the costly experimental phase were to find their way into the eventual solution. After all a great number of evaluation studies have already been abandoned for lack of interest in the results.

Thus even special support for innovatory initiatives remains inconsequential in the Federal Republic because on the one hand exceptions cannot be established on a permanent basis, and on the other hand there is no way of imposing results achieved as compulsory. What *has* happened is that the reform experiments of the past have provided work for a greater number of staff interested in reform. Now that, under the impact of a policy of financial cuts, financial support for innovation is no longer available, this opportunity has gone too.

The special status of the professorial staff, and the freedom of research and instruction as guaranteed by the constitution, are another aspect of the historic heritage with a strong influence on the attitude towards innovation in German higher education. Freedom of instruction and research is first of all to be understood historically as one of the civic rights successfully fought for in the age of enlightenment during the transition from a feudal to a bourgeois society. In the history of Prussian-German higher education, however, this right of freedom appears from the start as a privilege granted to the universities by the state. Since in the course of the ensuing development the professors became the sole beneficiaries of the privileges granted to the universities, the freedom of instruction and research developed into a personal right attached to the individual members of a special class, ie of the professors. The degeneration of republican principles has always been characteristic of German political culture. Perverting a right to freedom into a state-controlled privilege is in that sense only a token of a more general tendency. Since the West German state considers itself to be fully in the tradition of previous state forms, there is no need to be surprised to find the highest court of the Federal Republic stating in 1973 that, in university committees deciding on matters of research and instruction, the professors as a group must have an absolute majority.

Before this, some universities had been given constitutions which had taken into consideration the growing importance of other constituent groups (students, other teaching staff, non-teaching staff). These developments were effectively stopped by the 1973 pronouncement. Legislation and court rulings in the last few years have accentuated this tendency. Thus the universities are again characterized by an increasing range of artificial hierarchical relationships propped up by dubious legal norms. Under the present restrictive conditions those who are privileged in this system tend to be primarily concerned with defending their prerogatives, while those who are dependent feel a growing need to conform in order to avoid risks. But how are innovations to be made without risks? Here is another example: on their appointment professors are at the same time accorded a general qualification to teach. Is it surprising then that it is a rare exception indeed if a professor seeks didactic advice in order to improve his university teaching?

Finally, when talking about the resistance to reform in higher education, it is also necessary to talk about the special ideology of German academic establishments. There is a saying that the German middle class, after its political failure, has surrendered its critical reason (ie the heritage from the period of enlightenment) to the German university. The cultivation of a critical rationality in the individual was replaced by a blind belief in science and the universities were encouraged to develop excessive claims for their activities. Consequently the universities have never conceived of doing anything else but what, in their understanding, is academic work and academic education. No other demands have been made of them either. The history of the German university is characterized by recurring attempts to preserve its identity. In the nineteenth century the university dissociated itself from the education of teachers (with the exception of grammar school teachers, who were to receive an academic education because they prepared pupils for university). The upgrading of colleges of technology to full academic status had to be implemented against the unyielding resistance of the universities. Today it is the question of the integration of the (non-academic) education at the 'Fachhochschule' and the university that meets with strong resistance on the part of the universities. For educational tasks beyond the narrow framework of their understanding of academic work (eg further education) the universities are badly prepared. An 'Open University' as developed in Britain would be in flat contradiction to nearly everything that could qualify as a living tradition in the development of German higher education.

'Die Hochschuldidaktik ist immer wieder in der Gerfahr, statt die Studenten auf das Niveau der Wissenschaft zu bringen, die Wissenschaft auf das Niveau der Studenten zu bringen:' which in translation means teaching in higher education is always in danger of moving science to the level of the students rather than the students to the level of science.' This is an authentic remark from the 'fringe' of the 'Westdeutsche Rektorenkonferenz' (Standing Conference of the Principals of the West German Universities). It is hardly two years old and can be certain of widespread agreement within the universities.

PROSPECTS

I have given an outline of some of the traditions in the development of German universities that seem to me to affect the capacity for reform under present conditions. I do not claim that this is in any way a comprehensive treatment of all the tendencies and problems in the West German higher education system. I see my contribution as an attempt by a 'professional reformer' to develop a fuller understanding of the difficulties of his own work. The factual basis of my analysis could only be sketched somewhat summarily. There are many developments that could have served as exemplary evidence for the strength of and the interplay between the various factors detrimental to innovation in concrete situations.[2] A few final remarks should be devoted to possible future trends in the development of West German higher education.

Obviously the West German universities are also a sociological sub-system which is in constant change. However, in all those areas particularly interesting to the pedagogically motivated reformer the universities have remained rather antiquated. I do not believe that this is going to change in the future just because the idea is spreading that questions of teaching and learning deserve more attention than they have been given so far. On the other hand there are good grounds for the assumption that state and university cannot help making a number of rather fundamental changes in higher education in the not too distant future which are likely to open up, as some sort of side-effect, developmental possibilities within teaching and learning. These changes have to do above all with the transition phases from school to university[3] and from university to career.[4]

It is no longer the classical grammar school alone that qualifies pupils for university studies; in fact the classical grammar school does not any longer exist. The idea of a broad general preparation for studies in practically any subject had to be given up in favour of a comprehensive system of choices and specializations. The universities are now facing the problem of laying the foundations of scientific work in the respective fields themselves — a task far beyond what they have traditionally thought their function to be. This situation has — quite independently of the present economic crisis — arisen from the rapid development of the sciences. The problem of the transition from university to career, on the other hand, is directly connected with the end of economic expansion. Since the labour market will be less and less able to find appropriate employment for university-leavers the close connection typical of the German education system between university degree and career becomes questionable. There is less and less justification for end-of-study examinations qualifying someone for quite a specific career (eg as a teacher) if the chances of actually working in it are minimal. Moreover, in the foreseeable future in our country more and more students will have to be educated by fewer and fewer staff.

All this is putting pressure on the universities (and state planners) to modify their rigid study and examination systems. Opportunities for more differentiated and less rigidly controlled studies could be the result. From this might emerge the possibility of reaching some of the important aims of curriculum reform after all. It is true that no honest reformer will derive pleasure from the idea that he needs the economic recession as an ally to reach his goals. But since we have no influence on the economic framework of our activity anyway, let us without undue scruples understand our task to be this; with all the changes which the future is going to bring, to work towards the best possible conditions for instruction and learning in our universities.

NOTES
1 The history of the German university has been traced in countless publications. A comprehensive selection will be found in: Wiegandt, E. (1912) *Bibliographie der Hochschulpädagogik* Leipzig; re-edited Rieck, W. and Schmithals, F. (1981) Hamburg AHD
2 For more detailed information see: Schmithals, F. (Editor) (1981) Staat und Studium, Die Studienreformkommissionen — Eine Zwischenbilanz 1980/81 *Blickpunkt Hochschuldidaktik* 66
3 A detailed analysis of actual problems related to the question of access to higher education will be given in: Welzel, A. (Editor) (forthcoming) *Der Übergang Schule — Hochschule als didaktisches Problem*
4 The discussion of transition to career problems was much stimulated by a paper issued by Wissenschaftsrat: Empfehlungen zur Differenzierung des Studienangebots (Nov. 1978).

6 RECESSION, UNEMPLOYMENT AND STUDENTS IN GERMANY

Götz Schindler   Bayerisches Staatsinstitut für Hochschulforschung und Hochschulplanung

Before discussing the recession in Germany, one has to remember that it was policy in the 1970s to give as many people as possible the opportunity to attend university. As a consequence, student numbers between 1970 and 1980 increased from 410,000 to 825,000. During the same period, there was an 80% increase in the number of professors (1970: 13,400; 1980: 24,200). As regards teaching personnel as a whole, however, there was an increase of only 45% (1970: 48,200; 1980: 69,400). This means that the staff/student ratio deteriorated from 1:9 to 1:12 (BMBW 1981/82, p. 152). Moreover, since 1979 there has been virtually no increase in the number of teaching personnel, although the number of students at universities has increased by approximately 100,000 since 1979. In some Länder (States), staff vacancies have not been filled and universities have been asked to cancel courses (DUZ 1982, No.9, pp.26-27).

As regards cut-backs in buildings, the situation is even worse. Because of the soaring student numbers, universities were already overcrowded by 1980. At the beginning of 1980 the Federal government, which pays for 50% of new university buildings and basic equipment, was not prepared to tell the Länder governments how much it would be able to spend on new university buildings. Hence, during the next five years, only two-fifths of the planned new buildings will actually be built. The Federal government and the Länder governments finally agreed upon new buildings only for courses with good job opportunities for graduates (natural sciences and engineering). Even so, the Federal government will not be able to provide for its full share. In 1982 and 1983 it may contribute DM 900m instead of DM1.2b. Even in student housing, the recession has caused cut-backs in new buildings. During 1979 and 1981, the percentage of students living in dormitories decreased from almost 12% to 10% (DUZ 1982).

As far as unemployment is concerned, the general unemployment figure increased from 4.4% in 1975 (1m unemployed) to 5.4% in 1981 (1.3m unemployed). Unemployment among university graduates is a minor problem compared to general unemployment because the unemployment levels have been below the general unemployment figure: 1.5% in 1975, 1.9% in 1979, and 3.2% in 1981. In 1981 there were approximately 40,000 unemployed university graduates in Germany. But whereas the general unemployment ratio has had its ups and downs, the unemployment ratio among university graduates has been rising continuously over the last seven years (UNI 1981, p. 24).

It is not easy to determine what impact these developments have upon new and existing students. There is some evidence that factors other than recession and unemployment exert an influence. This conclusion may be drawn from certain inconsistencies to be noticed if one looks at the data available.

On the one hand the percentage of school-leavers who want to attend a university has declined from 76% in 1975 to 68% in 1980. Moreover, the number of student entrants has been rising much more slowly than the number of school-leavers entitled to attend a university. In 1975 there were 127,000 graduates from the Gymnasium entitled to attend a university, with 122,000 actually entering university, whereas in 1980 there were 168,000 Gymnasium graduates and only 139,000 student entrants (BMBW 1981/82, p. 104). Obviously, Gymnasium graduates feel disconcerted, because attending university no longer seems to guarantee entry to the profession of the student's choice. And there seems to be little doubt that job prospects play an important part in new students' choice of courses.The decline in the number of student entrants in teacher training from 33% in 1975 to 21% in 1980 is due to the fact that the number of new teachers employed has been declining sharply for financial reasons ever since the beginning of the seventies. Another example is the decline in student enrolments in engineering during the same period, which came about as a reaction to employers' warnings in the mid-seventies not to take up engineering at university because there might be too many engineers on the labour market before long.

On the other hand, however, there has been an increase in the percentage of student enrolments in the humanities, social sciences and economics (31% in 1975, 41% in 1980 (BMBW 1981/82, p. 112)) although the job prospects for graduates of these courses have been deteriorating. From this we may conclude that recession and unemployment among university graduates certainly has some influence on the Gymnasium graduates' decision whether or not to attend university and on their choice of course, but they obviously do so only for a minority. There has not been a marked change in students' reasons for attending university. Surveys show that between 60% and 80% enrolled on their course because they felt it would match their talents and special interest, and only a minority expected graduation from their course to open the door to high income and reputation (Griesbach, Lewin, Schacher 1977, p. 54; Müller-Wolf 1977, p. 62-63).

What has been changing since the mid-seventies is the students' opinion about what their future profession means to them personally. A survey shows that it is 'very important' or 'important' to 98% of students that they get the chance to apply their talents and capabilities in their profession; for 92% that they may do independent work; and for 87% that they may do their job by co-operating with others. Only 64% think that high wages are important and only 19% think that it is very important or important to be highly respected by others (Wildenmann 1980, p. A 11).

This is one of the keys to understanding student conduct. Unemployment and recession have an influence on student choice, but their influence is being intensified by a change in values which has been taking place among students in the 1970s. There is much frustration about job prospects. Only 10% think there will be no problem in finding an appropriate position; 40% are sceptical; 17% expect some problems; and 15% expect considerable problems (Framheim 1981, p. 109). But it is not only that there are problems in finding an appropriate job; it is the fact that by being unsuccessful in finding an appropriate position after graduation they feel excluded from their most important opportunity for self-realization. As a consequence students do everything they can to improve their job prospects, and work harder to get good grades than students did in former times. The average amount of time spent on studying per week rose from 41 hours in 1970 to 50 hours at the end of the 1970s (Kunow 1978, p. 26). Besides, competition among students has been increasing, and this is why most reject group-work: only 10% of them join with fellow students regularly to get prepared for classes and tests (Krause 1980, p. 97).

But student reaction to deteriorating job prospects is complicated by another factor. One of the latest surveys concludes that German students at the end of the seventies expected the university to contribute to the development of their personality but that the university was neither willing nor able to cope with this task (Framheim 1981, p. xvii). This is due to several reasons. First of all, according to a resolution passed by the Conference of University Presidents (Westdeutsche Rektorenkonferenz) the development of the students' personality should happen of its own accord. Thus they rejected the idea that universities should play an active part in this matter. Moreover, factors such as *numerus clausus*, the deterioration of the staff/student ratio mentioned above, the increasing specialization of courses, and regulations on courses and examinations which in many cases impose too many restrictions on the students' freedom of choice, make it almost impossible for most students to develop personality traits such as creativity, independence, ability and readiness to co-operate with others. As a consequence, what students feel they lack most is the relevance of courses to their lives.

REFERENCES

BMBW (1981/82) Grund- und Strukturdaten *Der Bundesminister für Bildung und Wissenschaft*

DUZ (1982) *Deutsche Universitätszeitung* 8, 9

Framheim, G., Bargel, T., Dippelhofer-Stiem, B., Peisert, H. and Sandberger, J.-U. (1981) *Studium und Hochschulpolitik* (Schriftenreihe Hochschule, No 39) Bonn

Griesbach, H., Lewin, K. and Schacher, M. (1977) *Studienverlauf und Beschäftigungssituation von Hochschulabsolventen und Studienabbrechern* Volume 2, Munich

Krause, Chr., Lehnert, D. and Scherer, K.-J. (1980) *Zwischen Revolution und Resignation. Eine empirische Untersuchung über die politischen Einstellungen von Studenten* Bonn

Kunow, J., Schloz, U. and Simon, H.U. (1978) *Wie motiviert sind die Studenten?* Mannheim

Müller-Wolf, H.-M. (1977) *Lehrverhalten an der Hochschule* Munich

UNI (1981) *UNI-Berufswahl-Magazin* 7, p. 24

Wildenmann, R. (1980) *Studentische Beteiligung an universitären Wahlen* (Forum des Hochschulverbandes, Heft 21) Bonn; pp. 1-43

7 A MARKETING PERSPECTIVE

J.G. Duncan   Queen Margaret College, Edinburgh

Demographic decline in traditional client groups and the vagaries of political economic policy constitute the two most potent academic and administrative problems facing universities and colleges today. The popular and educational press bear testimony to the varied efforts of institutions to cope with these problems: solutions which range from proposed staff redundancies to 'sales drives' to attract overseas students. Any educational institution is faced with three primary tasks in order that long-term survival and stability may be achieved. It has to attract sufficient resources — students, staff, research, finance; convert resources into products, services and ideas; and disseminate outputs to various consuming publics — industry/commerce, government, community. Marketing is the organizational process most concerned with managing mutually favourable exchange relationships between a responsive organization and its dynamic environment.

Despite the growing awareness and adoption of 'management-in-education' theory and practice, marketing has been singularly neglected in the British education field. Previous research (Duncan 1979) uncovered a wealth of American literature but a paucity of European material (Doyle and Lynch 1976a, 1976b) on non-profit marketing practice in education. This literature, while superficially demonstrating the applicability of theory to practice in an educational setting, singularly failed to grasp the complex dynamics of institutional practices. Marketing tended to be merely imposed upon organizational processes.

BASIC MARKETING METHODS AND TECHNIQUES
Many authoritative statements (Kotler and Levy 1969; Shapiro 1973; Kotler 1982) expound the applicability of business marketing techniques to non-profit service organizations in society. A paper at the MEG Dublin Conference (Duncan 1981) attempted to illustrate the proposition in tertiary education at the level of 'naïve marketing' practices. Kotler (1976) has long asserted that the 'marketing principles for non-profit organizations are the same as those for profit.' He maintains that the marketer must identify key markets, employ market segmentation, analyse consumer behaviour, develop an appropriate product mix, evolve strategies, etc. All of which can be applied to education and would be highly relevant activities for universities and colleges. Benson Shapiro (1973) argues that four key concepts summarize the basis of marketing thought and action in a non-profit environment:

1 The *self-interest* aspect of the exchange in which both the buyer (student) and the seller (college) believe they are receiving greater value than they are giving up.
2 The *marketing task* which stresses the importance of satisfying customer needs (students and employers).
3 The *marketing mix*, the elements of which are the tools that marketers use, eg product, price, place and promotion.
4 The idea of a *distinctive competence* in which the university/college concentrates on what it does best.

These, then, are the guiding principles which have to be embraced by educational institutions in the 1980s and beyond.

Figure 7.1 provides a simplistic illustration of the two levels of marketing interaction: (a) *macro-level* — society and those political, social, technological and economic institutions that will influence the release of resources for the educational purposes; (b) *micro-level* — the organizational activities and processes harnessed to meet the externally derived influences, opportunities and needs. In summary, the crucial parameters are:

a   The dictates of UGC/SED/DES/local authority policy, finance, course development and allocation (also CNAA).
b   The strength of the institution's internal resources allocation.
c   The 'opportunity gap analysis' of new markets — technology, skills, employment, leisure patterns.
d   The ability to attract a variety of student groups.
e   The institution's relationship to research bodies/employers/users.
f   The uniqueness/relative advantage of courses.
g   The flexibility of its organizational structure to meet change.

These areas have been singled out as they constitute the university's or college's own largely 'controllable marketing variables' — courses, place, price and promotion. The diagram serves to illustrate and define the various important sets of interdependent relationships that a university/college has to manage. Figure 7.2 identifies those specific organizational tasks and activities to which marketing methods and techniques can be usefully applied.

Organizational Audit
Organizational audit consists of three parts (Duncan 1979): evaluate the organization and its environment; evaluate the organization's 'marketing system'; and evaluate the major areas of 'marketing activity'. The audit should reveal the major practices, problems, threats and opportunities facing an institution and subsequently lead to more effective academic and administrative planning.

Markets
Markets are defined and segmented into meaningful target groupings as the basis for strategy and the composition of a courses mix. The dynamic nature of the markets has to be reflected in any decision-making procedure (bearing in mind the lead-lag nature of the educational product). Such basic questions as '*who* are our students, *where* are they located, *why* do they come to this institution, *what* do they seek, *how* do they decide (or are influenced) to come here', are the crucial information areas for any future plans. All information from both internal and external sources that will aid modification of current courses and the design and development of future curricular requirements is then purposefully monitored.

Products (Courses)
Courses are the educational raison d'être of an institution and in the past these often unique offerings evolved and modified themselves slowly. In complete contrast to marketing tenets, course development often arose from an internal (ideas) process devoid of any external (market) considerations. New strictures imposed by UGC/DES/SED, CNAA, and other bodies now require these incipient ideas to be

FIGURE 7.1 Educational institution (non-university sector) in total societal marketing environment

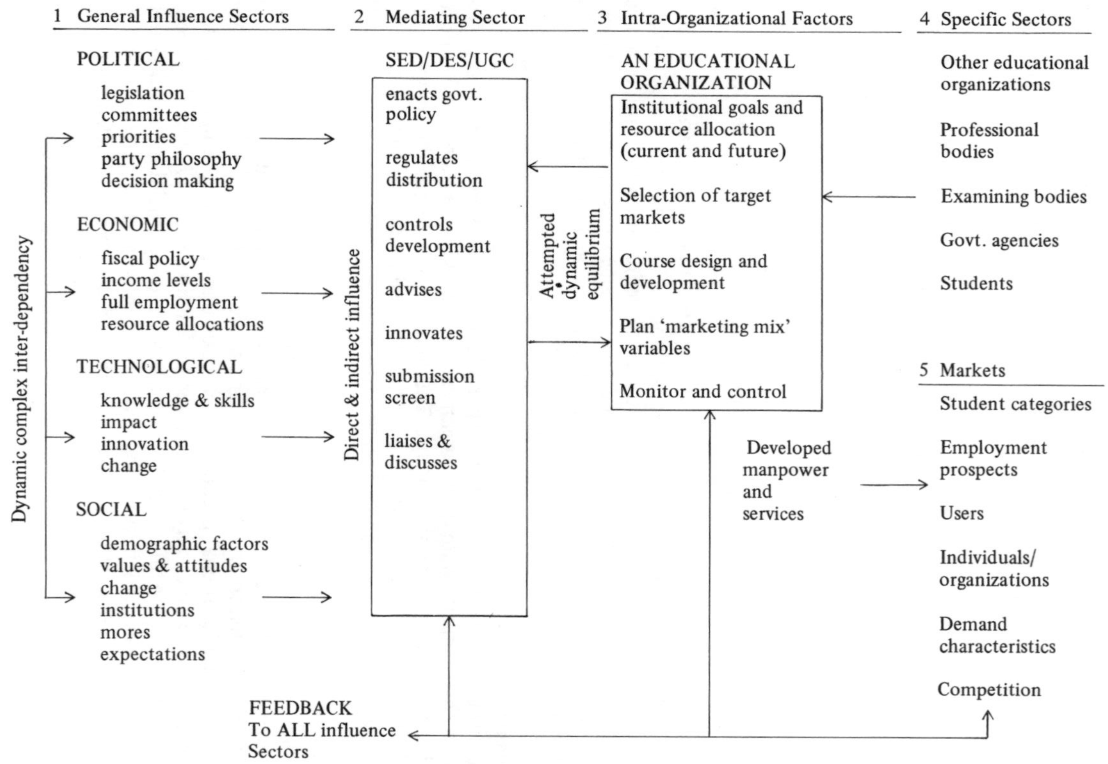

1 General Influence Sectors	2 Mediating Sector	3 Intra-Organizational Factors	4 Specific Sectors

1 General Influence Sectors

POLITICAL
legislation
committees
priorities
party philosophy
decision making

ECONOMIC
fiscal policy
income levels
full employment
resource allocations

TECHNOLOGICAL
knowledge & skills
impact
innovation
change

SOCIAL
demographic factors
values & attitudes
change
institutions
mores
expectations

Dynamic complex inter-dependency

FEEDBACK
To ALL influence Sectors

2 Mediating Sector

SED/DES/UGC
enacts govt. policy
regulates distribution
controls development
advises
innovates
submission screen
liaises & discusses

Direct & indirect influence

3 Intra-Organizational Factors

AN EDUCATIONAL ORGANIZATION
Institutional goals and resource allocation (current and future)
Selection of target markets
Course design and development
Plan 'marketing mix' variables
Monitor and control

Attempted dynamic equilibrium

Developed manpower and services

4 Specific Sectors

Other educational organizations
Professional bodies
Examining bodies
Govt. agencies
Students

5 Markets
Student categories
Employment prospects
Users
Individuals/organizations
Demand characteristics
Competition

FIGURE 7.2

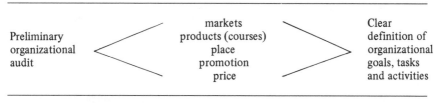

| Preliminary organizational audit | markets products (courses) place promotion price | Clear definition of organizational goals, tasks and activities |

partially validated by some hard market data and tempered by the dictates of political and economic reality. Whatever 'form' a course may take, one can further analyse the 'product concept' in terms of three levels:

1   *Core product* — the identification of the basic need being sought, eg to study biology, physics, philosophy, history, sociology (fields of knowledge).
2   *Tangible product* — the degree or diploma being offered and associated with the additional 'features' such as *level* (ordinary, Honours, higher), *brand name* of institution studied at (Edinburgh, London, Oxford, Cambridge).
3   *Augmented product* — the sum total of all benefits and costs that the student receives or experiences in obtaining the degree or diploma.

The 'product concept' in marketing directs our attention to all that 'happens' to the student in his/her effort to obtain the tangible product, eg decision to take a course, to receive instruction, to experience learning, to sit examinations, to comply with various rules and regulations, to conform in behaviour, to discipline activities. The course is perceived quite differently by the student and by the institution.

Product Mix
Another problem for an institution is that of 'adapting its course range to the needs of the market which is likely to be increasingly seen as the central issue' (Doyle and Lynch 1976). A courses mix (see Figure 7.3) consists of *items* (individual courses) and *lines* (groups of related courses) while the matrix also illustrates the ideas of courses' *width* and *depth*.

FIGURE 7.3 Course Mix

Course line	Basic qualification	Post-qualification
1	Dip. Science Degree (Ord), (Hons)	
2	Arts Degree (Ord), (Hons)	PG Diploma
3	Degree in Management Science (Hons)	MSc
4	Dip. Public Admin.	

(width ↑↓)

←————————————— depth —————————————→

The academic policy decision on a courses mix will be made at three different levels: the specific course for specific market segments; the course line — to add, delete, extend, modify; and the mix — the 'total composite' offered by the institution. By increasing the 'width', an institution will hope to capitalize on its reputation and skills in *present markets* whereas an increase in the 'depth' of a line may entice *students with varying needs*.

Promotion
The current and varied formats of promotion employed by institutions bear testimony to the seriousness of this marketing activity. Promotion encompasses the planned/unplanned, the intended/unintended; the whole pervasive web of communication raises many issues and touches on recruitment, employment, corporate image, etc. It may be useful first to relate marketing communications to an institution and its market, as in Figure 7.4.

FIGURE 7.4

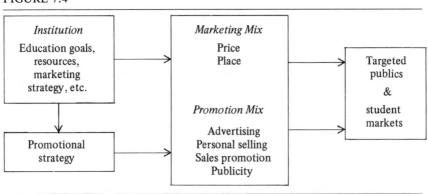

The inter-relationships of promotion to marketing strategy are shown. Promotion attempts to overcome consumer ignorance by providing information concerning the institution, its courses and all its diverse activities and services. It also attempts to overcome consumer inertia by using *persuasion* to create a favourable psychological association between the establishment and its varous publics. Both these promotional functions have to be distinguished clearly when formalizing promotional objectives.

There is today an increasing awareness that institutions have to diversify their communication systems — the old 'supermarket-approach' of saying 'here we are and these are our courses' is a prescription for doom. There are too many attractive products vying for the customers' attention. One current line of inquiry which is helpful to the promotion strategist is to look at the evidence of student motivation and decision making. The useful data produced by Whitburn et al. (1976) coupled to the model of Doyle and Lynch (1976) shows that key time variables exist which constrain the prospective students' 'search' strategies and, at certain stages, the influence exercised by different reference groups. A communication plan would be to aid this process with appropriate 'messages' and design activities to reinforce/aid selection.

Overall Plan

Marketing is about people, organizations and their structures, and the complex of relationships that exists between them (Matthews and Blackwell 1980). The key to an organization's survival and growth lies in the fact that there must be a continuous development of new and improved courses. Even in education, gone is the confidence that established courses will maintain their dominant market position indefinitely. Accepting the dynamic and problematic realities of the educational environment, the 'opportunity analysis' can, as Baker (1978) suggests, be organized around two dimensions of change against which markets and courses (their innovation/design/ development) may be considered.

FIGURE 7.5 A grid for opportunity analysis

Educational Markets		Course Design and Development		
	New Market	New application of 'existing' courses	Market extensions	Diversification 'new users'
	Extended Market	Course 'conversion'	Adaptional 'modular options'	Course line extension
	No Change	Present courses mix position	Curricular 'reformulations'	Replacement of courses
		No change	Improved	New

Figure 7.5 makes it clear that course development is a choice of three basic matching strategies: move into less familiar markets, eg from vocational into non-vocational; move into less familiar courses, eg design a course unfamiliar to present mix; and move in both directions simultaneously, ie new course and new markets (greater risks or pay-off). The current richness of curricular innovations (modules, options, etc.) coupled to the 'availability pattern' (full-time, part-time, sandwich, block-release, etc.) gives the maximum flexibility necessary to meet the diverse market and consumer needs.

In addition to these matching strategies, a college can adopt the following marketing approaches to course planning:

a *Undifferentiated* — a course is offered to a 'mass' student market rather than to any particular segment. This is seen as the academic equivalent of the 'product approach' exemplified in 'our course is as good as anyone else's' to all prospective students, eg a straightforward pass degree (but does recognize different ability levels).

b *Differentiated* — offering several versions of a course (ordinary degree, Honours in specific areas), each one designed to suit both varying student abilities and different segment characteristics and needs.

c *Concentrated* — here the emphasis is on a particular market segment and
focuses all the resources upon developing and marketing a course suited to its
needs, eg a degree in educational marketing.

These permutations are a means of achieving some measure of predictability over
a college's 'educational future' and hence viability. Although there is a great difficulty
in forecasting the 'life expectancy' of any new course, the preceding framework does
allow for a more rational planning approach through which the 'great ideas for a
course' can be critically and systematically screened.

Higher education is not simply in the business of instrumentally providing
knowledge and skills to suit manpower needs, but is also addressed to the 'social
benefits' of a wider community. Innovative course development can only come from
the broader, outward-looking and integrative approach which realizes that 'real life
problems and their solutions' are not neatly packaged within disciplinary boundaries
(Meadows and Perelman 1977). Once an institution has formulated its strategy to
the point of target market selection, a programme must then be formulated to
serve the wants and desires of the chosen segments.

GENERAL ISSUES AND PROBLEMS
The cursory overview presented here indicates that the transferability of traditional
marketing concepts, techniques and methods to service organizations is highly
problematic and the theoretical frameworks are under-developed (Lovelock 1979;
Walters and Taylor 1979). Marketing applied to education (Newbould 1980; Doyle
and Newbould 1980) tends to be prescriptive in nature and there is little
acknowledgement of the substantive difficulties which arise in transfer. The public
and humanistic benefits of education do not easily accommodate into a marketing
framework traditionally associated with a materialistic ethic.

Educational establishments do not, per se, practise marketing, and what may be
carried out in some institutions is a rudimentary and, at best, fragmentary attempt to
copy the commercial world. There is a paradox: university and college academic
departments of marketing exist, yet their expertise is rarely used. If marketing is to
become an accredited activity in institutions of higher education, marketers have to
understand the dynamics of organizational life before an effective contribution to
academic and administrative planning can be made. Academic disciplines are sub-
cultures and not merely administrative categories (Trow 1975; Lockwood 1979) and
hence the rational managerial processes are restricted by the nature of the academic
task and its resources.

Baldridge and his fellow researchers (1978, 1975) further highlight the
organizational complexities — great goal ambiguities, the use of problematic
technology, fragmented professional groupings, diffuse plural decision making, etc.
The essence of marketing activity, the design and development of new products/
services, and the battery of rational methods and techniques (Andrews 1975; Midgley
1977) are inapplicable to 'educational products'. The creation of new courses and their
attendant complexities relies upon a compound of professional judgement, creative
insights, practical experience, well-defined value systems and orientations to
specialized fields/domains of knowledge (Becher and Kogan 1980). Bernstein's
(1971) apposite point about the 'subordination of previously insulated subjects or
courses' neatly illustrates the array of pressures which can exist when attempts at
collaboration of a multidisciplinary or interdisciplinary nature arise in new degree
planning. Marketing's central tenet of 'know the customers' needs/wants' is

inordinately difficult to translate in practice; most educational consumers are either unaware of a need or possibly unable to articulate one. This state of affairs necessarily perpetuates the 'product-orientation' rather than the classic consumer orientation. Given these dimensions in academic life, marketing practice is often relegated to such convenient and 'soft areas' as student recruitment and institutional publicity.

Heightening competition between colleges and universities is already apparent in such tactics as lowering or abolishing the formal entrance qualifications, offering part-time first degrees, wooing sixth formers by giving them pre-university residential experience, X's polytechnic's Hitchhikers' Guide to Education, etc. The promotional excesses discredit thoughtful marketing application — over-zealously produced adverts and prospectuses, coupled to glowing accounts of the live and vibrant social and educational experiences which await the student, too often create illusions and false expectations. It is interesting to note the growth of 'alternative' student-produced calendars and prospectuses in this area. The American literature is replete with examples of tasteless and excessive tactics employed in recruitment and promotion (Lovelock and Rothschild 1980). Having alluded to only a selection of pertinent issues and problems (Berry and Kehoc 1980), it is obvious that much research (Duncan 1982) has to be done before an appropriate transfer of marketing concepts and related techniques can occur. One can well understand the anathema engendered when an enthusiastic yet well-meaning proposal is mooted to 'market the university'. The preceding examples will serve as an aide mémoire for some of the underlying difficulties (Fram 1975).

CONCLUSIONS
Education and marketing are equally concerned with the future. Consequently some attempt at forecasting the key parameters has to be made. Woods (1976) succinctly expresses the issue: 'success for a college is whether it managed change or was managed by change'. The consistent theme here is a belief that with the prevailing and future uncertainties confronting education (King 1979), individual institutions will have to adopt a 'marketing orientation' in order to survive the vicissitudes of change. Marketing is not, however, a panacea, neither is it the modern-day search for an educational Holy Grail: 'constantly looking for the elusive student who will satisfy members of the faculty by being the most academically capable and well prepared of any students in the country ...' (Mudie 1978). Such positions are indefensible and reflect an academic version of 'tunnel vision'. Educational marketing is a 'holistic' mode of thought. It has to permeate the entire organization's activities and any successful marketing strategy and planning will have to be based upon objective research data and 'not upon the quicksands of tradition', departmental whims or intuitive academic hunches. Central questions, like those posed in an organizational audit, are designed to remove the host of 'impressionistic data' that often gets bandied around as quasi-knowledge of college affairs. According to de Moor (1978), future tertiary education will vary as to levels, objectives, students, teaching methods and teachers. Leavitt (1968) describes how 'management myopia' can so easily develop within an enterprise and states that 'the primary business of every business is to stay in business. And to do that you have to get and keep customers.' This applies, with even greater urgency, to educational institutions in today's and tomorrow's markets.

Universities and colleges will have to re-assess their relationship with their educational environments and equally re-appraise their current course offerings (Lynch and Hooley 1980). Two fundamental issues remain: first, for any institution, the estimate of *future demand* for its courses and services; and secondly the recruitment of students to fulfil its organizational goals. Both these problems come under the purvue of marketing.

Becher (1975) argued for a marketing orientation and stressed the needs of consumers in higher education. In 1982 survival in the educational market place is a traumatic yet novel experience to those socialized into the 'expansionism ethos' of post-Robbins (1963). Lord Vaizey's (1978) rejoinder about the broader student clientele and the wider social benefits to the old, handicapped, women, unemployed and unskilled, offers an educational and marketing challenge of social relevance to lifelong and recurrent education concepts. Innovation implies change — in academic and administrative practices, in attitudes, in new patterns of educational demand and experiences — and the marketing function has a role to play in this process.

REFERENCES

Andrews, B. (1975) *Creative Product Development* London: Longman

Baker, M. (1978) Limited options for marketing strategies *Marketing* June, pp.23-27

Baldridge, J.V. et al. (1978) *Policy-making and Effective Leadership* San Francisco: Jossey-Bass

Baldridge, J.V. and Deal, E. (Editors) (1975) *Managing Change in Educational Organizations* Berkeley: McCutchan

Becher, R.A. (1975) Curriculum change in an age of consumerism *Times Higher Educational Supplement* 183, 18 April, p. 11

Becher, R.A. and Kogan, M. (1980) *Process and Structure in Higher Education* London: Heinemann

Bernstein, N. (1971) On the classification and framing of educational knowledge, in Young, M.F.D. (Editor) *Knowledge and Control* London: Collier-MacMillan

Berry, L.L. and Allen, B.H. (1977) Marketing's crucial role for institutions of higher education *Atlanta Economic Review* 16 July-Aug., pp.24-31

Berry, L.L. and Kehoe, W.J. (1980) Problems and guidelines in university marketing *American Marketing Association Educators Conference Proceedings* Chicago, Ill.: American Marketing Association

Doyle, P. and Lynch, J.E. (1976a) University management in a changing environment *Higher Education Review* 8 (3) 15-28

Doyle, P. and Newbould, G.D. (1980) A strategic approach to marketing a university *Journal of Educational Administration* 28 (2) 254-270

Doyle, P. and Lynch, J.E. (1976b) Long range planning for universities *Long Range Planning* December, 39-46

Duncan, J.G. (1979) *Marketing a College in the Non-University Sector of Higher Education* MEd dissertation, University of Edinburgh

Duncan, J.G. (1981) Marketing of higher education: an institutional dilemma *Marketing Education Group Annual Conference Proceedings* Dublin: College of Marketing

Duncan, J.G. (1982) Social marketing in action — the new course development process in education *20th International Congress of Applied Psychology* University of Edinburgh, workshop paper

Duncan, J.G. On-going Ph.D. research, University of Edinburgh

Fox, F.A.K. and Ihlanfeldt, W. (1980) Determining market potential in higher education *American Marketing Association Educators Conference Proceedings* Chicago, Ill.: American Marketing Association

Fram, E.H. (1975) Marketing revisited *College Board Review* 94 Winter, pp.6-8, 22

King, E.J. (Editor) (1979) *Education for Uncertainty* London: Sage

Kotler, P. and Levy, S.J. (1969) Broadening the concept of marketing *Journal of Marketing* January, pp.10-15

Kotler, P. (1976) *Marketing Management* 3rd edition, London: Prentice-Hall, p.496

Kotler, P. (1982) *Marketing for Non-Profit Organizations* 2nd edition, London: Prentice-Hall

Leavitt, T. (1968) *Innovations in Marketing* London: Pan Books, p.9

Lockwood, G. (1981) *An Analysis of the Planning Process in 1968-73 in the Context of the History of the University of Sussex and the Management of the University* DPhil thesis, University of Sussex

Lovelock, C.H. (1979) Theoretical contributions from services and non-business marketing *American Marketing Association Educators Conference Proceedings* O.C. Ferrell et al. (Editors) Chicago, Ill.: American Marketing Association

Lovelock, C.H. and Rothschild, M.L. (1980) Uses, abuses, and misuses of marketing in higher education *Marketing in College Admissions: A Broadening Perspective* New York: College Entrance Examination Board

Lynch, J.E. and Hooley, G. (1980) The university choice process *EAARM/MEG Proceedings* Edinburgh: Heriot-Watt University

Mathews, H.L. and Blackwell, R.D. (1980) Implementing marketing planning in higher education *American Marketing Association Educators Conference Proceedings* Chicago, Ill.: American Marketing Association, pp.1-5

Meadows, D. and Perelman, L.J. (1977) Limits to growth, a challenge to higher education *Prospects* 7 (1) 34

Midgley, D.F. (1977) *Innovation and New Product Marketing* London: Croom Helm

de Moor, R.A. (1978) Diversification of tertiary education in Western Europe *Reform and Development of Higher Education* Council of Europe, Slough, Bucks: National Foundation for Educational Research

Mudie, H.C. (1978) Identifying and expanding the desirable student pool *New Directions in Higher Education* No. 21, Spring. San Francisco: Jossey-Bass, pp. 7-22

Robbins Committee (1963) *Higher Education* Cmnd 2154 London: HMSO

Shapiro, B.S. (1973) Marketing in non-profit organizations *Harvard Business Review* Sept./Oct. 123-132

Trow, M. (1975) The public and private lives of higher education *Daedalus* 104 Winter, 113-127

Vaizey, John (1978) Post-compulsory education in the 1980s *Higher Education in Europe* Oct.-Dec. 3 (4) p.42

Walters, C.G. and Taylor, R.D. (1979) Contingency marketing and contemporary marketing management: a comparison *American Marketing Association Educators Conference Proceedings* O.C. Ferrell et al (eds.) Chicago, Ill.: American Marketing Association

Whitburn, J. et al. (1976) *People in Polytechnics* Guildford: Society for Research into Higher Education

Woods, B.A. (1976) *Application of a Marketing Model to a College Recruiting Programme* DEd thesis, University of Oklahoma

8 FLEXIBILITY IN COURSE PLANNING

Eric Hewton   University of Sussex

The recession has stimulated a search for economies in most institutions. Apart from seeking areas where direct cost cutting is possible (such as building and ground maintenance, support services, etc.), administrators and academics are now, more frequently, questioning the efficiency of the teaching process itself. Attempts to derive formulae by which to calculate costs per student or per course have increased in recent years, leading to the demise of those courses which attract only a small number of students. The reasoning behind this is simple. The unit cost per student is calculated on the basis of:

$$\frac{\text{Cost of course}}{\text{No. of students}}$$

As many costs are fixed or semi-fixed (eg lecturers' time, space, heating, administration, etc.) then, within limits, the more students on a course, the lower the unit cost. This does no more than reflect a key economic concept: 'economies of scale'. Certainly, if the number of students on a course is increased there will also be some increase in variable costs, such as the time devoted to marking, the additional costs of registration and record-keeping, etc., but the unit cost curve will generally tend to fall, until it reaches a critical point at which new 'lump-sum' costs are incurred when, say, an extra teacher is needed or extra accommodation has to be provided. An economist would seek to increase the size of a course until this critical or optimum point is reached. An administrator operating under practical, rather than theoretical constraints, must compromise and impose a cut-off point below which a course is regarded as no longer viable. Thus we frequently hear that courses, or sometimes options within them, will no longer run if student numbers fall below 20, or 12 or 8 or whatever figure is regarded as economically and sometimes politically acceptable. Less often do educational factors influence these decisions.

There are, however, good reasons why a shortfall in student numbers should not result in the immediate closure of a course. All of these reasons can be challenged but together they add up to a case which at least needs to be considered.

— A fall in student numbers may be only a temporary set-back; changes in market influences occur frequently and are often hard to predict. Demand for a particular course can change dramatically over a three-year period.
— Once a course has been stopped it is often difficult for administrative, financial or political reasons to start it again. Damage may also have been done to its reputation and credibility.
— The educational experience which students receive on a small course can be equal to or even superior to that received on a large course. It can be more comfortable for some students; there may be closer personal contact between students and staff and students themselves may feel part of a more closely knit group.
— Choice itself can be good from a course marketing point of view. The more

courses on offer the more the likelihood of attracting a wide range of students and enrolling those who might have chosen, or been forced, to go elsewhere.
— Choice may also be good from an educational standpoint. Some students, at least, might welcome the opportunity to help tailor courses.

Whereas many academics and administrators would agree with some, if not all, of these arguments, questions of economy will generally defeat supportive action. But need this be the case? Two investigations at the University of Sussex — one completed and concerning undergraduates, and one ongoing and concerning a postgraduate course — suggest otherwise. Some aspects of these studies, and in the former case the action taken, will now be described.

THE USE OF TEACHING TIME
The investigators — in both cases small groups of academics — avoided what they considered to be the unit cost trap. Instead they asked: what amount of teaching time does a single student generate? This is not an unreasonable question, as a student enrolled upon a course in any institution brings to that institution a fee which would not otherwise be earned. This fee, in part at least, contributes towards the cost of teaching. There are many ways of proceeding from this basic premise but one is to relate the time generated by each student to the formulae already adopted by the institution for calculating departmental, staff/student ratios and standard weekly or yearly teaching commitments required of individual staff. These vary across institutions and departments within them but such calculations are becoming increasingly common.

At Sussex, for instance, in one of the departments concerned, the teaching ratio adopted for the year 1981-82 was 13.5:1. It was also expected that a lecturer would teach for 270 hours. It can therefore be argued that the teaching time that one student generates is

$$\frac{270}{13.5} = 21 \text{ hours}$$

In other words, if only one student enrolled on a particular course he or she would be entitled to twenty-one hours of the lecturer's time over the whole year whereas two would be entitled to forty-two hours, three to sixty-three hours, and so on. If three students were required to do three options within a course taught by separate lecturers then each lecturer would have to ask: how best can I use twenty-one hours to teach three students?

UNDERGRADUATE TEACHING
The completed study within one undergraduate department started from the premise that on each of the courses in one year of their programme a student generated twenty minutes per week teaching time. The way this figure was arrived at need not concern us here; it was based upon standard formulae used to calculate teaching allowances for arts and social science departments but it was also subject to modification by individual departments according to their own needs, provided the maximum allowance was not exceeded. On the basis of this allowance it was possible to see how each lecturer, responsible for a particular course, used the total time available. All lecturers were interviewed and a schedule of their teaching patterns was completed. It became clear that although lecturers differed from each other

slightly in the way they organized their teaching time, they were all influenced by traditional practices long since accepted in the department concerning size of groups, modes of teaching and length of sessions. For instance very few lecturers, even on courses with a large number of students, ever lectured or even used large (eight or more) seminar groups. Most taught only small groups of up to five and nearly all tutors provided some individual tutorials. The following are two examples both relating to different second-year option courses.

TABLE 8.1 The generation of teaching time

	No. of students	Teaching time generated per 10 week term	Teaching methods used	Actual teaching time per term
A	15	15x20 mins x 10 weeks = 50 hrs	(a) 5 groups of 3 for 8x2hr sessions	80 hrs
			(b) 2x30 min individual tutorials	15 hrs
				95 hrs
B	7	7x20 mins x 10 weeks = 23hrs 20min	(a) 9 x 2 hr seminars	18 hrs
			(b) 2 x 30 min individual tutorials	7 hrs
				25 hrs

The examples in Table 8.1 indicate that a small course need not necessarily be less economical than a larger one, indeed it can be the opposite if an appropriate teaching mode is chosen. In the former case the lecturer concerned felt continually under pressure and was having trouble keeping up with his research. It would have been simple, but probably unhelpful, to suggest that he should double the size of his teaching groups. Instead the researchers drew up a table showing how all members of the department used their teaching time, then posed a number of questions concerning the variables involved in the situation and finally constructed a number of hypothetical models indicating alternative uses of time.

The figures came as a shock to many members of the department. For the first time it was apparent that, overall, lecturers were exceeding the department's allotted teaching time by over 20% — a fact which helped to explain why many were feeling considerably more strain and pressure than they had in the past. A departmental meeting was called to consider some questions: What are the advantages or disadvantages of teaching in groups of three rather than six or more? Are different skills required for teaching in large groups? Do students necessarily prefer smaller groups? (Subsequent research revealed that students were often divided on this question, sometimes finding larger groups more stimulating.) Need a session last for two hours? Need there be eight sessions per term? Need the lecturer attend every session or stay for the whole time? Are individual tutorials always necessary and need they last for thirty minutes each? Might students double up, and learn from each other in tutorial sessions? If a total switch to teaching in larger groups was not an acceptable solution might not a mixture of modes involving the occasional large seminar, a few small group tutorials and one or two individual tutorials be feasible? Finally, might there not be a possibility of combining, for part of the time, two or three small courses which covered some common ground? As a result of the investigation some major changes in course and teaching organization within the department were introduced and at least one small course which looked in danger of being withdrawn was reprieved and redesigned on more economical lines.

POSTGRADUATE TEACHING

The second study of the use of teaching time, which is still continuing, is again raising questions about the traditional way of organizing teaching. Normally, postgraduate courses in the department concerned are based upon a series of seminars for twelve students. To provide the same series of seminars for only six students is clearly uneconomical — so what are the alternatives? Ideas which are at present being discussed and are likely to be tried in the future include: fewer seminars, shorter seminars, student-led seminars, more detailed and directed reading, concentrated study workshops, etc. The discussion and thinking through of these possibilities has also led to the drafting of a new proposal for an MA by independent study which could be viable even if only two or three students enrolled.

The argument for a degree in independent studies is as follows. Each year there are a number of students who would prefer to do, and are capable of doing, an MA without following set courses. They either have particular areas of interest which they wish to pursue; or none of the existing courses exactly fits their needs; or the course structure does not enable them to arrange their study time to meet attendance requirements.

One possibility might be for them to pursue a further degree by research (eg an MPhil) but this is not attractive to all students. It generally means concentrating upon one issue or problem which is analysed in depth. Normally the student works entirely alone and is supported by one supervisor. The product is usually a thesis of 40,000 words or more.

An MA by independent study would differ in several ways First, it would probably be assessed on the basis of three pieces of work (projects or short dissertations) which might, but need not necessarily, be connected. Secondly, the student could have several supervisors over the period of study according to particular needs at particular times. Thirdly, if two or more students were to follow this route at any one time, it would be possible to define certain broad areas of common interest (concerned with, for instance, research methods or philosophy) and provide directed reading, some specially prepared materials and occasional joint supervision or workshop activities. Students would also be expected to join MPhil and DPhil research students for regularly held research seminars.

Suppose that five out of the 100 or so students currently engaged in taught MAs in the department were to opt for an independent route. Together they would generate 105 hours of teaching time. This could be used in various ways, but one possibility is set out in Table 8.2.

The scheme would have a director of studies and lecturers taking part would receive a teaching allowance according to their contribution — as they would on any taught course in the department.

It might be argued that such a scheme, involving a great deal of independent

TABLE 8.2

Each individual student has a 1 hour tutorial every 2 weeks over 3 terms. 5 students x 15 hours	= 75 hrs
There would be 6 x 2 hr seminars (2 per term) on reseach methods	= 12 hrs
1 (possibly residential) 3 day workshop would be held during which students would discuss their work with each other	= 18 hrs
	105 hrs

work, would not be suitable for the majority of graduate or undergraduate students. This may be true but it does not affect the main argument here — that courses can sometimes be built on the resources generated by even a few students. This is not necessarily a direct challenge to the prevailing view that courses should be designed and students enrolled; rather it offers an alternative for the educational entrepreneur to build 'small businesses' in the gaps between the larger course concerns. There are a number of benefits that could accrue from pursuing this approach. First, it would provide for some students whose specific educational needs would not otherwise be met. Secondly, it would enable a more flexible use of resources. Thirdly, it would help to prevent precipitous decisions being taken on the future of seemingly uneconomical courses. Finally the need to re-think teaching strategy could lead to the more imaginative use of teaching resources, including the more creative use of self-instructional media and materials.

9 AUDITING STAFF ENERGY

Graham J. Stodd   Bishop Otter College, West Sussex Institute of Higher Education

The strategy presented here is a possible way of reconciling the conflicting demands of teaching, research, development, administration, committee work and autonomous staff activity in institutions of higher education. It results from practical involvement in the problem, rather than a detailed review of the relevant literature, although this will eventually take place. It is assumed that all institutions have a finite amount of accountable staff energy available for these activities and that this total is the product of the hours in a working week, the weeks in a working year and the number of full-time equivalent staff. The term *staff energy* is used rather than staff hours to describe the total commitment a tutor might be reasonably expected to give to an institution, rather than just face to face teaching contact. Although this approach is quantitative, the aim is to achieve a qualitative creation of 'space' to enable each of the conflicting activities to take place.

The strategy is presented only in broad outline, because it is still being developed, but some detailed work has already been carried out on producing appropriate algorithms to support it. In order to be fully effective, this strategy would need to be supported by an interactive suite of computer programmes, available for use by individual staff, course leaders and senior management. This suggested strategy clearly opens up a broad debate about conditions of service, accountability and academic freedom: concepts that are identified here but not discussed.

THE CONCEPT OF STAFF ENERGY

Given an agreed length to a working week and year, it should be possible to calculate the total number of hours generated by all the staff (full-time equivalent or FTE) in an institution, and this represents the total accountable energy available to that institution for the academic year. It is possible to divide the total energy between teaching, research, development, administration, and committee work while also allowing for autonomous activity, unforseen contingencies and overstaffing. There is no implied priority in this order of treatment. The quantification exercise is essentially for management purposes, enabling decisions to be made. One made, the quantification of time to the individual activities becomes less important and in practice the balance between them might be different. The quantification exercise will have ensured that the institution and its individual courses and staff are not over-committed.

EXCESS ENERGY

Many institutions will occasionally be over-staffed in terms of the norms implied by the DES staff/student ratios and the calculation of the total accountable energy will include this excess energy. Rather than allow it to be dissipated, it may be appropriate to quantify it as a separate sub-total and to allocate it to specific activities or projects, which might not otherwise be carried out within the routine work of an institution. Projects such as a piece of market research, the development of non-course specific self-instructional teaching materials, the computerization of some field of activity, a laboratory or workshop re-organization, might all qualify for allocations of energy from this excess sub-total. In management terms, this means that positive gains will have resulted from the over-staffing, enabling it to be justified more easily.

TEACHING

Institutions might decide to allocate somewhere between 40% and 65% of their total accountable energy (excluding the excess) to teaching, recognizing that the other activities will need to take place in the remaining proportion. Before allocating this energy to particular courses, it may be wise to create a pool of energy to service the general administration of whole programmes of study and to bolster up unviable courses. The general administration of programmes would be concerned with such things as staffing, timetabling, estimates, resource allocation, internal and external assessment and evaluation. The pool of energy might also support a limited number of unviable courses, which an institution, after careful consideration, had decided to maintain.

The allocation of energy to individual courses is probably best done by the use of an algorithm, incorporating a base unit of staffing energy. This represents the amount of teaching energy notionally available to an individual student in a single week. It is calculated by dividing the total teaching energy (excluding the pool) by the total of full-time equivalent students and further dividing that by the number of weeks in the students' academic year. If a greater degree of sophistication is required, it is possible to weight the base unit according to different years of study or to different programmes, allowing more intensive teaching on some courses or programmes than on others.

The resulting base unit can then be incorporated into an algorithm, to calculate the teaching energy available for any individual course. It is first necessary to establish a course ratio, which is the proportion an individual course occupies in a timetabled week (eg a four-hour course in a sixteen-hour timetabled week would have a ratio of 0.25). Multiplying the base unit by the number of students on a course, then by the course ratio and finally by its duration in weeks will give the amount of teaching energy available to that course. The course leader, together with the teaching team, will then need to decide how this total of teaching energy will be allocated to individual team members. In doing this, they will need to take account of five discrete activities, which all consume staff energy in any course: namely adminstration, preparation, teaching contact, follow-up and pre-course study.

Administration includes such things as: producing course lists and teaching timetables; arranging visits, speakers, films and teaching accommodation; controlling staff, student records and budgets; monitoring assessment and evaluation. Preparation is concerned with the preparation or revision of lectures and other teaching and learning resources, pre-course planning meetings, familiarization with resources and rehearsal of teaching strategies. Teaching contact is the time actually spent in face to face contact with students, and will include lectures, seminars, small groups and individual tutorials, with tutorials demanding far more teaching energy than lectures. Follow-up may involve marking, other assessment procedures and record keeping, as well as participation in evaluation. Finally, pre-course study is concerned with any study of texts, papers and other resources, which tutors need to do, in order to prepare themselves for the course. The balance between these five teaching activities will vary for individual courses, with some courses demanding greater contact añd others greater administration. The crucial point is that, whatever the balance, the total amount of teaching energy, produced by the use of the algorithm, may not be exceeded.

Having decided on the amount of energy to devote to each of the five teaching activities, the course leader and team will need to agree on the most appropriate allocations of energy to individual tutors. Some teams may decide to allocate the energy equally to all tutors, whereas other teams may decide to give some tutors a greater involvement than others, leading to a more cost-effective use of staff energy.

RESEARCH AND CONSULTANCY

Although research and consultancy are felt to be important, some institutions find it difficult to create the space necessary for them to flourish. Parallel with the allocation of a proportion of energy for teaching, institutions would allocate a proportion, though a smaller one, for research and consultancy. Individual tutors would then be invited to make bids for portions of this research time by producing a detailed account of their previous year's research activity. They would give a cumulated summary of the time spent on each research activity, supported, where appropriate, by referees, publications, log-books, etc.

Institutions would then need to decide on the level of recognition they wished to give to each of these bids. Where the research activity was felt to be essentially for the benefit of the institution, a 100% recognition might be given to the time claimed; where the research activity was essentially for the benefit of the individual, a 10%, 20% or 30% recognition might be given; or an appropriate intermediate level of recognition might be given. This, of course, assumes that teachers in higher education will see their professional activity extending beyond their accountable activity into evenings, weekends or vacations. This retrospective analysis of the previous year's research activity would produce a total energy requirement for the subsequent year and an institution might then need to adjust its initial allocation of research energy either upwards or downwards. This use of the retrospective analysis has the advantage of being based on proven past performance and will create the necessary space for subsequent research and consultancy to take place.

DEVELOPMENT

Many institutions are in a state of constant change and it is vital that adequate staff energy be set on one side to support future development. Such energy will be used to support the three categories of staff development, programme validation and course implementation.

The majority of staff development will probably involve either full-time or part-time attendance at some other institution. As with research, a judgement will need to be made concerning the level of support and this will again be concerned with the relative balance of benefit between the institution and the individual. For example, on each year of a two-year part-time course, a tutor might be allowed a 50% relief of work load if the benefit were deemed to be essentially with the institution, whereas the allowance might be as low as 10% if the benefit essentially lay with the individual; again, the assumption being that tutors will work in evenings, weekends and during vacations. This strategy should ensure that there is positive support for tutors involved in part-time study.

The validation of new courses is extremely time-consuming, involving meetings, consultations, library and market research, visits, document drafting, plus considerable meditation and informal discussion. In order to ensure a satisfactory allocation of energy, it might again be appropriate to use an algorithm, supported by a suitable base unit. The base unit would represent a notional allocation of time to develop one week of a course for one student and institutions would need to debate the most appropriate level at which to set this base unit. They might, for example, decide to allow exactly the same amount of time to develop the course as would be needed to teach it, or they might decide to double, treble or quadruple this figure. In terms of quality, validation is time-consuming and the quadruple figure might be the most appropriate level.

Having decided on the size of the base unit, exactly the same algorithm as that used to allocate teaching energy could be used, taking a target number of students instead of actual student numbers. Clearly, the larger the target group, the larger the amount of development energy, because programmes for larger target groups will often have parallel courses or options each demanding separate development. Again, as with allocating teaching energy, the development energy would need to be differentially allocated to individual members of the team, recognizing their level of involvement. This strategy for allocating development energy should ensure that institutions create sufficient space to give quality to their developments.

The third category of development energy is that used in the implementation of new courses, because the first year a course is run it is likely to need additional staff energy to that produced by the use of the teaching energy algorithm. As with establishing a base unit for the development of new courses, institutions will need to establish a base unit for their implementation. In the case of development, it was suggested that a quadrupling of timetabled time might be appropriate, but in the case of implementation a half of the timetabled time might provide a sufficient topping up. The precise amount of implementation energy available for a particular course would be defined by calculations similar to those used with teaching energy. The resultant figure will be added to that achieved by the use of the teaching energy algorithm, producing an enhanced amount of staff energy for that course in its first year of operation.

ADMINISTRATION

There are many administrative activities which consume staff energy in institutions: including subject area responsibility, registry, counselling, careers advice, library, recruitment, interviewing, residential responsibility and educational technology. There are, however, differences between institutions as to the extent to which these activities consume academic, as opposed to administrative, staff energy. In allocating energy to support each of them, it is suggested that institutions should define a notional amount of time, per student per term, for each activity, as it affects students. For example, an allocation of 0.5 hours per student per term, to cover subject responsibilities in an institution of 1,500 (FTE) students, would produce an annual total of 2,250 hours, which might be set against the annual work loads of a number of heads of subject. Institutions might well conclude that 0.5 hours was an inappropriate allocation for this activity and decide to raise or lower it. Using this approach, it should be possible to calculate a cumulated total to cover all the administrative energy of an institution.

COMMITTEES

Committee work can be extremely demanding in its energy requirements and institutions may find the following strategy helpful. It is first necessary to quantify the annual total of timetabled man-hours for all committees in an institution (eg a committee of six, meeting six times a year for an average of two hours consumes seventy-two man-hours). Institutions will then need to decide on the level of support for preparation and follow-up they wish to give to such timetabled committee work (eg the committee of six might be given a further 72 hours, 144 hours, 216 hours, or more, by way of support for their timetabled meetings). This notional amount of additional support should enable papers to be prepared and read before the committee met and follow-up tasks to be carried out. Clearly, for a committee to be really effective, institutions will need to allocate a significant amount of time for follow-up work.

It should then be possible to use a simple formula to allocate energy to individual committees. Some members of a committee usually contribute more to its work than others, and the allocation of energy to individual members of a committee should reflect their different levels of involvement. This strategy should certainly enhance the quality of committee work in institutions.

AUTONOMOUS STAFF ACTIVITY
Institutions will need to decide on the proportion of their total accountable energy they wish to reserve for autonomous staff activity, and such a decision may well involve professional associations. Having quantified the total for autonomous activity, institutions may decide to use a two-stage strategy, initially allocating a proportion equally to every tutor and then allowing individual tutors to make bids for allocations from the remaining time. Bids might be made to cover work as county or district councillors or as magistrates. Bids might also cover the writing of a book, service on national committees or other professional bodies, examining, or research not accounted for under the research heading. This autonomous activity is central to the richness of institutional life and it is vital that sufficient time is allocated to it. Finally the need for a contingency fund is self-evident but very important. As well as enabling institutions to respond to unforseen contingencies, it allows energy to be allocated to individual staff to meet them.

BALANCING THE BOOKS
The strategies suggested here should help institutions to reconcile the conflicting demands of a range of activities which consume staff energy. The final balancing of the books will clearly involve considerable adjustments of the energy allocations to each of the activities and may take a number of years to achieve. In addition to the global balancing of the books, individual tutors will receive allocations of energy under some or all of the headings, cumulating to a full accountable work load.

Although in one sense the strategies advocated imply a tighter control over the way academic staff operate, it may be that they also result in a greater freedom. Many institutions are undoubtedly over-committed, trying to do too many things with their finite total of staff energy. The suggested strategies would result in a rationalization of activities, providing space for staff to gain satisfaction from their work.

10 PATHFINDING EVALUATION

G.M.E. Blom and J.M. Verbeek   University of Amsterdam

RECESSION IN THE NETHERLANDS

Recession is a recent phenomenon for Dutch universities. Our institution, the University of Amsterdam, was first confronted with it in 1980 when staff reductions began to be made as a result of budget cutting. The graph in Figure 10.1 shows the change in academic staffing since 1960 and the expected reduction up to 1987. The curve demonstrates a sharp cut in staff employed after 1980.

FIGURE 10.1 Number of academic staff: University of Amsterdam 1970 - 1987

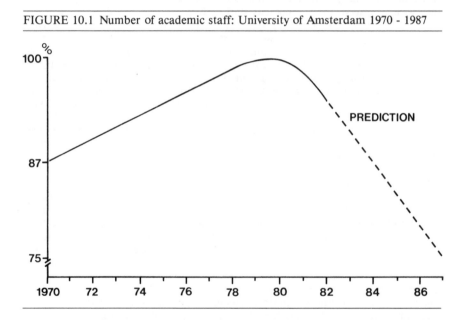

The year 1982 is significant, for new legislation forced the universities to develop four-year curricula out of the previous five or six-year ones, and set a maximum of six years to a student's time at university. Such governmental reductions will oblige the universities from 1982 onwards to provide two types of curricula in parallel — one for students on the old, five or six-year courses and one for those on the new shorter courses. Combined with the staff reduction this raises the question of how to maintain the necessary standards of quality in the curricula.

We present here an approach to evaluation in which standards of quality are dominant, and are seen as a means of finding new ways in which academic departments may develop. First we describe the formal status and financing of academic departments in Dutch universities, and then explain our approach to evaluation. Finally we discuss a few examples of departments which have evaluated their educational activities.

THE PLACE OF ACADEMIC DEPARTMENTS

A department, usually discipline-centred, has two main tasks: to run a curriculum in order to certify students; and to carry out a research programme and report on it. A Dutch department is financed from four possible sources:

1. Money given by the university for educational purposes, the amount being proportional to the number of students enrolled.
2. Money from the university for research purposes, recently on specific conditions, and, to a smaller extent, proportional to the number of students.
3. Money from state research foundations, mainly for pure research.
4. Money from private institutions and firms for contract research — mainly applied research.

The most important central control mechanism consists of the power to shift money from one source to another. Within the same national budget the Minister of Education planned to shift money from 'university' to 'research foundations'. Apart from this, no university has any financial autonomy whatsoever. The Ministry have to agree all payments made by the university. Departments can explore the free market of contract research, but it is estimated that only about 12% of university expenditure on research comes from this source. This system is best summarized as in Figure 10.2.

FIGURE 10.2 System of departmental finance

Source	Delivered by	Purpose	More/less important in 1984	Output
State	University →	Curriculum (i)	Less	Qualification of students
		Research (ii)	Less	
	Research foundation →	Pure research (iii)	More	Pure research
Private →	Third parties →	Applied research (iv)	Unpredictable	Applied research

STATE CONTROL : (i + ii) + (iii)
UNIVERSITY CONTROL : (i + ii)
DEPARTMENTAL INITIATIVE : (i + ii + iii) + (iv)

In the near future student inflow to universities will be limited by a ministerial decision and students will be distributed amongst universities by a national ministerial board.

Patterns of Competition

Assuming a department strives for a more stable and growing income, it follows, from what has been said above, that it is involved in several patterns of competition. First, within the same university, departments compete when of comparable discipline (historical versus political sciences) in order to attract as many students as possible. Contributing to the attractions of a department are: high status of the academic field, student preference, characteristics of curricula, good chances of later employment, and the widening of conditions for admission. Competition for research funds from the university favours co-operative research work with many publications, and with a high potential for social and industrial innovation. Departments with such research accommodate well to university policy on research, as they do to national research programmes.

Secondly, departments compete with departments of the same discipline in other universities when research programmes are presented to national research foundations for financial support. It seems to raise their chances if departmental members take part in the administrative tasks of these foundations, and if they become members of editorial boards of journals. There is, furthermore, the competition to get as large a population of students as possible each year among those who enrol to study the discipline. The total admissions for every university will, in future, be set by the Minister.

Thirdly, departments compete with research institutions for finance and for contract research. However, they feel hampered by their dual task: besides research, they spend a lot of time on educational duties, whereas research institutions only perform research activities.

Status and Legitimation

The position of a department depends basically on the size of its budget and its stability. Usually the aspirations of the department and its members go beyond the limits of the budget: more money is needed to develop real long-term research programmes. Most departments feel an urge to improve their financial condition, the more so when recession strikes and decreases in budgets dominate all perspectives. Competition becomes rough sometimes. The most important aspect of the perception of the department's position is its legitimation: the legitimacy of its existence; in management terms, the legitimacy of its budget. The recognition of various values expressed by the actions of a department affects the views of students, academics, management and relevant persons outside the department. It is helpful in obtaining a favourable position if people believe a department to be doing well: at least as well as other departments with respect to important academic and educational values. Attention is drawn to its unique contribution to the discipline, to good solutions of difficult problems, and to special features. Interdisciplinarity of curricula and research programmes can be of such value.

The process of departmental legitimation consists of demonstrating to others its right to exist and the legitimacy of its budget. Part of the acknowledgement depends on the presentation of good plans for development. According to Mahoney, the value-related perceptions of one's position are by no means always concordant with the observed reality and can be much manipulated. In describing the history of the publication of his book,[1] he makes it clear that a close look at discrepancies between scientific idealism and observed reality of scientific practice was not appreciated by fellow scientists. Since recession tends to promote scrutiny, the resemblance of ideals and reality seems to provide a sound basis for the development of a department when it has to compete with other departments.

Following Mahoney we see the importance of two forms of legitimation. A discipline, or its organizational counterpart, the department, qualifies students according to the standards of the discipline, and its research outcomes accord with standards defined by disciplinary values. We would add that the students must also be qualified for future jobs, and research outcomes can be as useful for non-academic interested parties as they can be academically. Departments have yet another way of improving their position: universities each have a policy and identity which they want to realize, and they depend, of course, on constituent departments pursuing institutional aims.

The exact content of these various value patterns is not important at present, as long as we are aware of their existence, and their role in legitimation. Thus, although academic responsibility is the first and best known factor of legitimation, there are other grounds on which the position of a department can be legitimated: it can try more strongly to accommodate university policy, and hence provide a bigger contribution to the university's identity (the University of Amsterdam, for instance, sees itself as a source of stimulation to the city and its region). Or it can try more directly to fulfil students' needs. Interesting subject matter, treated in a stimulating way, and leading to qualifications and good employment opportunities, may raise the student intake. Scientific work can sometimes be made useful for non-academic outsiders with a high interest in academic results (as are labour unions, for example.) Research that leads to industrial and commercial or social development is highly regarded, as are the students who can be employed without extended in-service training. If competing departments are rather backward in expressing these values in education and research, people will notice their own department's usefulness, and thereafter decisions might be favourable towards it. It might attract more students, experience friendly administrative treatment in the university and pick up research contracts; and departments well-equipped from other sources are more respectable when it comes to the dispensing of funds from the national research foundations. 'Unto them that hath, shall be given.'

It is difficult however to attend to all these multiple interests at the same time. Keeping high academic standards is frequently enough of a problem, and serving any other interests is possible only if ways can be found to integrate them. Being educational scientists, and given that education commands a 30% share in departmental finance, we draw attention to the evaluation of courses and curricula and call it *pathfinding evaluation*. In a time of recession, evaluation is particularly important in order to detect detrimental effects at an early stage. Without evaluation, the effects of recession might bring about a policy of the 'trouble-shooter' variety, without any overview, without any knowledge of cause-effect relations, and without specific goals and directions for the development of the department.

PATHFINDING EVALUATION

Evaluation can very well suggest ways of improving a department's position and legitimation as a result of inquiry into educational matters. A central viewpoint in pathfinding evaluation should be that issues *related* to the educational programme must be covered as well as the programme itself. It should provide:

— Detection of problems of effectiveness and of the quality of education.
— Suggestions for policy making regarding education.
— Contributions to the legitimation of a department's position

In designing our evaluation practice we made use of the views of three writers: Stufflebeam (1971, 1974), whose decision-orientated evaluation is based on comparison of educational activities 'as planned' with activities 'as performed' (it takes into account context variables and observations of learning activities and results); Parlett and Hamilton (1976, 1977), who say that evaluation should be 'illuminative', should present a picture of the whole, and solve complex problems and questions for those affected; and Stake (1967, 1973, 1974), for whom evaluation should be responsive, start from the need for information, and demonstrate how the values and standards of the people involved are expressed in educational activities.

Although we are indebted to these authors, we feel that a combination of their views is not quite enough. We need a strong basis to work from, a way of describing educational activities that is useful to students, staff and evaluators and the department. Part of the description itself should be the illumination of the educational tasks; observation should pick up suggestions for improvement; reports based on description and observation should cause no suspicion, and should clearly expose alternatives for policy. Observation is to be understood as a name for all the methods that may produce the required information.

We developed 'study-task descriptions' for these purposes. Students have to perform tasks in order to learn from them. Tasks are completed and assessed. Some tasks are specifically designed for assessment after the execution of previous tasks. Study-task descriptions contain:

— A list of student activities in proper order.
— The content of the activities, such as subject matter.
— The characteristics of the study situation; the level of prior knowledge required.
— The educational pre-requisites such as books, instruments.
— The time period in which to perform the task.
— The expected results and means of assessment.

A study-task description includes the issues and values of importance to a discipline and to a department. A study-task design is the concrete form in which these values are made operational. In particular, the criteria used in assessment embody these values.

Observation of study-tasks can reveal the problems encountered by students and teachers when they operate according to these values. Comparison between the description of the study-task and its execution shows specific instances where practical problems have arisen. Observation of students and teachers at work can reveal reasons for discrepancies, suggestions for improvements, and leads for research in educational and related literature.

Stages in Pathfinding Evaluation

We usually become involved in evaluation by request, sometimes a specific one, more often a general one, eg what could we do to assist in educational matters? We then proceed in five stages.

First, our orientation into the discipline and its department starts with reading all available written material about the content, aims and objects of the curriculum and its courses. We are also interested in general information about the state of affairs in the department, the way it distinguishes itself from other departments, its research activities, its financial structure, its development, its structure of decision making and its pattern of dependence on external decisions. Our questions to the inhabitants of a department about such matters tend to produce statements on certain values concerned with disciplinary craftsmanship, the speciality of a department usually being defined in such terms as 'interdisciplinary' or 'society related' or 'problem orientated'. We know that in later stages such values will be seen in the designed study-tasks and in assessment. In the evaluation, educational practice must be interpreted in the light of such values. The orientation is finished when we construct a plan: it may be a plan for the reconstruction of courses; it may be an evaluation plan; or it may be a hybrid containing both in close connection. The plan takes into account things learned about a department's position and its legitimation; it is specifically designed to improve these.

All this differs from the usual evaluation approach. Pathfinding evaluation relates student learning activities to the other levels of organization of the department. It tries to answer questions about how learning activities reflect the values of the discipline and of the department; how they relate to education and research activities; what help might be found in co-operation in education and research with external persons; and on what conditions the support of the university could be gained.

Our second stage is a description of educational activities in terms of the required tasks and sub-tasks for students and tutors. A curriculum as well as a course is a series of study-tasks, accompanied by teaching tasks, and by the end-tasks of students for assessment purposes. A task-description gives as detailed a picture as is needed; by division into sub-tasks one can choose the descriptive entity at will. In difficult cases we described single activities in as much detail as we could observe.

The task-description then shows:

— What students achieved before entering the course.
— The aims and objectives of the course.
— Learning activities as designed in order to reach these goals.
— Teaching activities as designed to increase the quality and effectiveness of learning.

Thirdly, the task description of a part of the curriculum or of a course is then used to design observation of learning and teaching. We want to know if the task was clear to the students, if they could find materials, if all the appropriate steps were taken, if the time was sufficient, if the tasks were relevant to them, if enough aids and cues were given. Teaching staff are also questioned, on subjects such as learning difficulties, the need for more and better materials, and problems of guidance and assessment. After these facts and opinions have been collected we make our interpretations. We judge the consistency of study-tasks with teaching tasks, and with the aids in the learning situation. We compare our observations with the design, and with known views in the educational literature. We estimate the relevance of the course or curriculum with respect to the values of the department and the discipline: we investigate where, and how, in the study-tasks these values are incorporated, and what was actually achieved in learning. We sometimes find that educational goals are set too low; in other cases, even with proper goals, we have found that the teaching tasks did not confirm these goals, and therefore did not confirm the values of the department.

The result of the evaluation is then presented to all the people involved, students and teachers, together with departmental officials. The former are mostly interested in efficient and relevant education, the latter in ways of improving education in such a way that the values of the department register more clearly in the course. The clear expression of important values in the course may provide the department with the necessary arguments when it comes to competition with other departments of the same discipline. The presentation of outcomes is described here as if it were simply one step; actually it is a recurrent activity, a frequent evaluative stimulation rather than a neat final report. In this way illumination of the problems encountered helps students and teachers to make their next task more realistic, and enables departments to change courses or curricula at short notice in order to improve the quality and relevance of education.

Discrepancies usually appear in several categories:

— Study-tasks are not performed as designed.
— The design of the task does not stimulate students to meet the required level set by the goals.
— The goals and aims do not correspond to the values of the department.
— The values expressed in the course do not serve the interests of the department, since they do not contribute to the legitimation of its position.

A deficiency in one of these ways usually leads to trouble in other respects.

The fifth stage is to formulate advice. Such advice to a department and its members may be based on specific surveys of the educational literature, discussions during the earlier stages of the evaluation, and comparisons with other similar departments.

Advice must then be translated into the design of tasks: study-tasks for students; teaching tasks and structuring for staff members; decision schedules for the department's board; and evaluation tasks for all those involved, in order to keep track of the changes.

Examples of Pathfinding Evaluation
Limited space prevents a full discussion of our work, but we have chosen a few examples of departments in a bad enough position to enable us to extrapolate into the recession-ridden future. They are characterized by understaffing and insecurity.

The first example is the Interfaculty Department of Environmental Science, (IDES). In its educational programme there was a series of twenty lectures on widely varying subjects, followed by a three-month period for project work. Student groups could work on their own to produce research reports, instructional programmes or other products of the activities of scientists. The students' backgrounds were widely differing, representing all disciplines, hence the group products were inter- or multi-disciplinary. Both students and department had complaints: the lectures were not as effective as they would have wished, the projects too often failed to be productive or relevant. It was from this point that evaluation started. Our orientation focused on the following problems.

— The object of IDES was obscure: staff were interviewed to determine a common denominator but they produced no consensus on a body of theoretical knowledge, on methodology or on the kinds of problems to be tackled.
— Financially the department only survived because of student intake and a small surplus budget to develop the department. Student enrolment was

to decrease, partly because of the complaints mentioned.
— The level of autonomy of the department was the lowest possible: a council of representatives of a large number of other departments supervised IDES.
— Departmental members held pessimistic views on future development; although environmental science had to be interdisciplinary, they could not institutionalize patterns of co-operation with other persons in the field.

The evaluation plan initially omitted the lecture series because changing it would not coincide with the policy of the supervisory council. The student projects were evaluated first, lectures in the following years, and the entire educational programme at the end.

Task descriptions were made for project work in the form of models of the working procedures of students. Some of the procedures let the students survey the Amsterdam region for environmental problems. Another procedure let them confront the results of their projects with the opinions of involved persons and parties, as well as with the opinions of environmental scientists. Students learned to work with the models and the evaluation showed their high productivity and enthusiasm, as well as that of the staff and other persons involved. For the department, the project results showed legitimate and highly relevant research attempts that paved the way towards co-operation with groups and institutions in society as well as with scientists. The department, as part of the evaluation, derived from the project reports various ideas for further investigation into the formalization of methods and the extension of the project outcome. Staff members became more optimistic, and students started to advertise the course to fellow students. The department was able to define its objectives in an exemplary way to the supervising council of the university. In the following years, the evaluation was extended to the remainder of the educational programme.

The position of the department was put to the test on four occasions.

1   A first run at reprogramming all Dutch higher education in 1976 caused problems: environmental studies were an attachment to the curricula of all disciplines. Departments dependent on student intake tried to keep as many students within the department's courses as possible and wanted to remove any other departments' courses. The evaluators advised the IDES to publicize environmental studies, and to use the evaluation outcomes as well as the results of a survey into the tasks of professionals in the field of environmental employment. Most curricula adopted the IDES course. Only four cases of conflict emerged, in which the central university Board mediated. All four cases were won, the clear reasoning resulting from the evaluation about the course showing its influence. In a short time the department got even more support from the university in the form of extra staff funding in order to deal with education-related problems.

2   A number of environmental studies courses developed nationwide. The dominant strategy was to develop a full-grown curriculum. The Amsterdam department objected to this approach because it was not consistent with the interdisciplinary nature of the field of knowledge. At the end of many years of complicated discussions and negotiations their view was acknowledged and their educational practice seen as a good example for other courses. In these discussions, the outcomes of the evaluation played a role: the connection of student reseach to departmental research activities, the establishing of

co-operation with institutions in the region and the interest shown by employers were all important.

3   The department succeeded, more than others, in getting research contracts; better co-ordination of research activities resulted in funds that otherwise would have gone to research institutions outside the universities. This contract research matched the research designs of the students' projects, although it was far more elaborate. Some projects were able to profit from the results; other projects took part in it. Evaluation has shown the attractiveness of a strong connection between the department's research activities, and the staff competence needed to guide student research efforts, the gain being less total staff effort.

4   In 1980/81 a recession set serious limits to all the university's activities. A re-shuffling of finance was scheduled, and staff decreases became a threat to all departments with weak legitimation. The Interfaculty Department of Environmental Science was not affected; it was acknowledged as a growing department and received extra staffing. The reasons for this university policy were the high expected student intake in future years and the agreement of departmental policy with university policy. In reaching this agreement, evaluation was important in as far as it made university policy clear to the department by translating it into educational terms. The evaluators also took care to inform the University's Board about the development of the department. The stable state of this department after several years of development was caused to a great extent by its transfer to a more favourable legal position with greatly increased autonomy. This shift became possible because of its successful development.

The second example deals with evaluation in the Interfaculty Department of Educational Science. In this case we will focus on the methods of pathfinding evaluation. The department was founded by several faculties within social science, and recruited its staff from these faculties for half-time commitment. It was not backed by the Minister for Education, who did not favour its growth and who channelled funds to other departments of educational science in remote universities. However, each collaborating faculty of social science in the University of Amsterdam contributed from its own budget and this allocation was matched from central university funds. Their major stronghold was a well-organized group of schools willing to co-operate, representing a cross section of the entire range of educational forms and types. It was believed that this group and its co-operation with academic research workers could counteract the minister's feelings about where the money should be spent. In the curriculum of the new-born department was a course in which students learned to design research proposals for grants from the National Research Foundations. The proposals had to take into account practical relevance, the state of affairs in educational science, methods of operationalization and practical constraints. The course was planned in five steps: orientation to the problem and preliminary problem-formulation; presentation of the proposal to four experienced researchers; presenting problem analysis by comparison with relevant literature and relevant case studies; choice of research strategy and operationalization by explaining supporting arguments; presentation and defence of the proposal to a panel of teaching staff acting as the research foundation. Students worked in interdisciplinary groups, interdisciplinarity being a major characteristic of the course and an important attribute of the department. On a national scale, much discussion amongst mono-disciplinarians was devoted to the nature and methods of educational interdisciplinary research. Future support from the university and from constituent faculties depended, to some extent, on successes in interdisciplinary courses and research. We reasoned that unravelling the mysteries of interdisciplinary education would foster the legitimacy of the department's position. The objectives of the evaluation were as follows:

— The enhancement of learning and teaching processes (effectiveness and relevance).
— The preparation for decisions about profitable forms of teaching and studying.
— The illumination of views on interdisciplinarity.

The quality of the courses had first to be evaluated. This involves appraising the consistency between the main elements of the course as designed and as executed: and the elements are, according to Glaser, goals, student tasks, teaching tasks, situational help, and assessment.

In describing and observing the elements of the course, all the activities of the students in the initial part of the course were noted. Their initial goal was to get acquainted with the problem field. This involved sampling articles and books as listed; tracing discrepancies between the author's views and reality as observed; discussing outcomes with peers; accumulating topics for further discussion and re-shaping these as scientific questions; doing a preliminary check on these questions with respect to 'openness' for research; reporting findings in five to ten pages; defending this paper, and reconstructing it afterwards.

Questions concerning the following were then put to each student and to all four teachers:

— The initial clarity of the task.
— The relevance of the task.
— The measure of difficulty of the task.
— The use of aids.
— The performance of the task, including time taken.

In addition to asking questions, we observed behaviour:

— Organization and execution of practical supervision and tutoring.
— Reaction of students to teachers and tasks.
— Students' efforts to raise the quality of their own products and of their peers.

The evaluators held discussions with the department's Board about evaluation issues, and with teachers about task descriptions and interpretation of observations. Task descriptions were made before the execution of a task and students welcomed them as 'advance organizers' that helped proper execution.

Among the outcomes of the evaluation, one is particularly dominant and of importance to the department. The course was tutored by four teachers from different disciplines. Students frequently formulated questions and views on the interpretation of the content of literature, on the essentials of scientific research (the issue of neo-positivism turned up many times), and on ways to define problems. The tutors kept up an appearance (without being aware of it, and contrary to their own opinion) from which students concluded that the tutors gave unanimous answers to problems. The tutors were in fact as much divided as were the students. This lack of unanimity did not become overt when it should have done, ie during educational activities, but was revealed after interpretation of the evaluation data. Consequently, discussions about scientific values and the norms of disciplines were suppressed, since no one had the right answers. This turned into a conflict when the tutors assessed the products of the first step in the course as positive whilst students held low opinions of their own work. The evaluators advised the department to plan course subject matter in future as a confrontation of disciplinary value systems when applied to real-life problems in schools. This advice was in accord with the nationwide discussion on interdisciplinary educational research. Other pieces of advice were to do with organization and implementation.

The department reshaped its policy in accordance with the outcomes of the evaluation. The university supported it by financing a survey of related problems in schools, and of the efforts of educational researchers in reaction to these problems. The competition with departments in other universities had no happy ending, however. Nowadays the department holds a much weaker position than it did when this evaluation was in progress. One of the reasons seems to be that its research programme was not strong, the staff keeping what they assumed was its best research work in their original department (half-time commitment). In this way, it is easier to get dissertations accepted; the tradition of a vested discipline offers better guidance.

Concluding Remarks

From evaluation in several departments (curricula and courses) we derived various leads for a framework for future development. The effects of recession (need for student enrolment, understaffing, competition amongst departments, dependency upon the central body of the university) indicate new courses of action from which several improvements could be expected.

First, students tend to select courses that give the best chances of future employment. Interdisciplinary and problem-oriented courses will be favoured. Interdisciplinary courses combine disciplinary approaches and methods as well as subject matter. However, not all combinations will stimulate satisfactory co-operation between disciplines or students.

Secondly, the understaffing of departments causes a shift from lecturing and tutoring towards the preparation and guidance of courses and towards the appreciation of help from external professionals (ie members of research institutions). The concentration of departmental tasks upon a smaller number of department members will force a department to combine tasks: education and research will be integrated, education and administrative tasks combined will call for co-operative groups of staff instead of individual segregation of responsibilities. This may increase efficiency as well as encourage adaptation to new tasks and new topics.

Thirdly, competition on a national scale amongst departments of similar disciplines necessitates legitimation of courses and research programmes. The co-operation of university departments with local organizations and institutions is found to be profitable. Learning tasks can be developed that incorporate professional fields of practice. These are valued by students and their future employers. Furthermore it introduces other people's problems into departmental research programmes, thus contributing to the acceptability of the whole research programme, if inter-relations can be shown between departmental research topics and topics from 'outside'.

Finally, the dependency of the university as a whole upon the policy of departments tends to give favourable administrative treatment to departments that maintain relations with external organizations, and contribute to the university's esteem and finance. Firm and established co-operation clarifies mutual interests and thereby fosters the legitimacy of both parties.

REFERENCES

Hamilton, D. et al. (Editors) (1977) *Beyond the Numbers Game* London: Macmillan

Mahoney, M.J. (1976) *Scientist as Subject: The Psychological Imperative* Cambridge, Mass: Ballinger

Parlett, M. and Hamilton, D. (1976) Evaluation as illumination. In Tawney, D. (Editor) *op.cit.*

Payne, D.A. (Editor) (1974) *Curriculum Evaluation — Commentaries on Purpose, Process, Product* Lexington, Mass: D.C. Heath & Cy

Popham, W.J. (Editor) (1974) *Evaluation in Education, Current Applications* Berkeley: McCutchan

Stake, R.E. (1967) The countenance of educational evaluation, Teach. Coll. Rec 68, . 523-540. In Hamilton, D. et al. (Editors) *op.cit.*

Stake, R.E. (1967) Towards a technology for the evaluation of educational programs. In Tyler, Gagné, Scriven *op.cit.*

Stake, R.E. (1973) *Program Evaluation, Particularly Responsive Evaluation* C.D.O. T.H. Twente Enschede Netherlands

Stake, R.E. (1974) Language, rationality and assessment. In Payne *op.cit.*

Stufflebeam, D.L. (1974) *Alternative approaches to educational evaluation: a self-study guide for educators* In Popham *op.cit.*

Stufflebeam, D.L. et al. (1971) *Educational Evaluation and Decision Making* Itasca, Illinois: Peacock

Tawney, D. (Editor) (1976) *Curriculum Evaluation Today* London: Macmillan (Schools Council Research Studies)

Tyler, R.W., Gagné, R.M. and Scriven, M. (1967) *Perspectives on Curriculum Evaluation (AERA monograph series on curriculum evaluation Vol.I)* Chicago: Rand McNally

11 STAFF DEVELOPMENT: A CASE STUDY ON STRESS

Anne Castling   College of Arts and Technology, Newcastle-upon-Tyne

This is an exploration of a single staff development initiative which had extensive implications for the life of the college over a continuous period. The stages of the process are linked with the literature and with those areas of research which either contributed to the climate of opinion within which the initiative could flourish or which provided authoritative support for decision making within the institution. The initiative was an investigation into causes of stress among college staff at a time of recession and an associated reappraisal of the internal dynamic of the organization. This led in turn to a programme of remedial measures.

In October 1980 the principal of the College of Arts and Technology responded to an 'alert' from a member of the team of student counsellors by asking the Staff Development Unit to investigate causes of stress in the college and to make proposals for remedial action. The principalship committed itself to giving full consideration to the unit's findings and asked them to include a programme of objectives for action in the short, mid and long term. The emphasis was to be on strategies for the successful management of stress, ie a positive approach to perceived problems.

The unit proceeded by:

a   Reviewing major changes in the college over the previous five years.
b   Analysing the current organizational structure of the college, particularly channels of communication (a research report was available on the latter).
c   Obtaining a broad picture of absence and illness patterns within the college from medical and administrative personnel.
d   Reviewing its own 'case load' in staff counselling over the previous two years.
e   Calling in as a consultant an applied psychologist from Newcastle University.
f   Reviewing recent literature and research findings on the causes and control of stress, particularly in the context of educational organizations.

The next stage was the setting up of a series of seminars for different groups of staff (senior teaching and non-teaching staff; heads of department; other ranks) for which briefing papers were provided and which required a detailed analysis of perceived stress factors within the individual's area of work to be carried out before the session. The seminar took the form of rôle-play vignettes illustrating 'typical' conversations between staff supposedly meeting informally in common rooms, during which an extensive list of stressors was drawn up, an exploration was made under the leadership of the consultant psychologist of the nature of stress and patterns of individual response, and lengthy consideration was given to coping strategies. This occupied the morning. An afternoon session was designed to discuss the issues raised during the morning at departmental and sectional level, looking particularly at ways in which stress might be prevented, alleviated or contained acceptably within each context. This discussion group then split into triads of people with similar concerns who sought to produce outline action plans for their areas of work. In the fortnight following the seminar these were discussed more widely within departments before being re-presented to the Staff Development Unit as the basis for its own presentation to Management. The unit offered a paper synthesizing its findings, together with a programme for action, to the college Management Consultative Committee for full discussion. The outcome of this was that each head of department or senior staff member with particular responsibility committed himself to a group of objectives for a period of two years within which, and at the end of which, progress would be reviewed.

The literature available for consultation was used both to seek a general orientation and to provide authority for the unit's proposals. Whereas reference to research underpinned the whole process, research findings were carefully balanced with the unit's own analysis of the actual college situation.

Having their background in counselling and personal development work, the unit's personnel were already familiar with the standard writings on stress and its management — Kahn et al. (1964), Lazarus (1966), Toffler (1970), Selye (1974), Cox (1978), Cooper and Marshall (1978), Spielberger (1979). These authors made it abundantly clear that organizations involved in rapid change would create levels of stress which individuals might find intolerable. The unit's survey of recent change in the college had produced a list of thirty-three significant and overlapping changes within the previous five years, including the progressive amalgamation of departments; the rerouting or replacement of a large percentage of senior staff including the principalship; the takeover of new buildings and abandonment of former 'homes'; the full range of curriculum development initiated by the various examination bodies; the development of distance and open learning schemes; the impact of new technologies; demands for courses with community involvement; the strengthening tide of Manpower Service Commission courses (and all that *that* entailed); and, of course, redeployment and retraining to avoid redundancy in the face of severe financial constraints. (By far the best attended staff development activity that year was the seminar on early retirement.)

It was not remarkable, therefore, to find evidence of tension-related illness and a high incidence of 'time-out' absences among staff, particularly in those departments with a high proportion of older staff, and those whose staff were doomed to commute from site to site like Der Fliegende Holländer of legend (and with no likelihood of reprieve). Ferguson (1980) draws attention to research which shows occupational stress to be a causative factor of a large range of illnesses, from coronary disease to rheumatism.

Many of these changes were not merely organizational but implied the necessity of changing relationships, whether among colleagues or towards students, a requirement to change attitudes and personal philosophies which staff might find disturbing and might (stressfully) resist. Gray (1979) points out that 'to have to change one's behaviour is the most threatening requirement of all', while Turner (1975) underlines the almost certain opposition to change from the individual who feels he might be entering 'unchartered territory where his shortcomings and incompetence might be exposed'. A useful summary of those organizational and curricular changes which imply a considerable reorientation of roles and relationships by the lecturer in further education is provided by Owen (1979) who emphasizes that technical, organizational and pedagogical changes will only develop successfully *after* changes in attitude — in other words, over time. By contrast the education service during this period was being asked to respond with growing rapidity and with fewer resources to change imposed from 'outside', including shrinking training and development budgets. The unit's perception of a considerable anxiety among staff about the speed and extent of change was in line with such promptings in the literature.

A second, related, cause of anxiety among professionals was indicated by research, namely uncertainty about aims and objectives, whether one's own or those of the institution and the resultant dis-ease if a mismatch between the two should become evident. (Put simply, how can I leave and seek more congenial work in the context of dwindling opportunities?) Turner (1977) describes this confusion of institutional goals when he refers to educational institutions exhibiting 'problematic preferences' whereby 'different members of the organization see different goals or give different priorities to the same goals or are unable to define these goals to the point where they have an operational meaning.' This sense of uncertainty will be aggravated in an organization which has grown out of the progressive amalgamation of institutions with differing aims; Shears (1982a) refers to the sense of threat experienced by staff whose teaching career has been entirely within one pedagogic tradition but who are then abruptly required to operate within a contrasting tradition with the influx of the non-traditional category of student.

Confusion concerning goals was certainly evidenced at the college and had been recorded in a report compiled in June 1980 for the principal by a researcher from Leeds University whose remit to examine the internal communication systems included the objectives: to assess staff reactions to already implemented and currently planned organizational change, and to determine the level of staff morale. In the conclusions of the report Edmands (1980) stated: 'The changes in long term organizational goals which most people feel must come are also disturbing to staff. There is a general uncertainty about what these goals are or should be.'

Research into stress frequently links uncertainty about institutional objectives and a confused perception by the individual of his/her own role. Pearse (1978) in a study of five thousand managers, named one strand of organizationally oriented stress as 'unclear job requirements', while thirty-five per cent of the sample used by Kahn (1964) complained of job ambiguity. Gray (1979) claims that in education 'role behaviour is never well defined but expectations are often considerable, unsure and not well negotiated.' (One wonders in passing about levels of stress among staff development personnel whose capacity to cope with 'role fibrillation' (Yorke 1977) is a requirement of the job.) Turner (1975) in his check list of questions which a manager in education should ask himself before embarking on a programme of change, includes:

a   Is there general agreement on the aims and purposes of the institution?
b   Are people clear as to what their duties and responsibilities are in terms of delegated authority for decision making?
c   Does the communication system work with reasonable efficiency?

The research report available to the unit identified inadequacies in these same three areas as being contributory to low staff morale and some forms of stress. Edmands (1980) stresses the relationship in a lengthy concluding passage:

'Most people feel unappreciated, overlooked and, in extreme instances, threatened by organizational changes which appear to devalue their traditional contribution to college life. Some people clearly feel they have skills which could be useful in meeting changed or changing needs and that these are being overlooked in the present atmosphere of "no" consultation.

'Members of the college staff feel that internal communications generally are poor, not because there is a lack of formal channels but because management and staff do not communicate in what is seen by staff as a meaningful way. There is a perceived lack of open two-way communication and, as a concomitant, a level of mistrust and suspicion which appears (to an outsider) to be inordinately high. Rumour and speculation abound and staff appear to mistrust management, senior staff and colleagues about issues which range from the most trivial occurrences to rather more serious matters of promotion and college policy.'

Whereas it should be noted that the Edmands survey was conducted mainly among junior grade staff, when the unit analysed feedback from management and senior staff the same confusions were apparent and the same sense of a lack of genuine participation in decision making was voiced. Moreover, senior staff felt themselves to be trapped between conditions imposed from above, and unrealistic expectations from below that they would make, communicate and implement rational decisions. Junior staff deplored the fact that senior staff no longer talked about education, only finance; senior staff regretted being no longer able to attend to educational issues, having perforce to devote their energies to managing declining budgets. Sadly, neither was hearing the other.

Other sources of stress strongly apparent in the feedback to the unit included inability to cope with the increasing volume of work demanded in the decreasing amount of time available for its completion — this was universal and is also emphasized by Turner (1975); and a resentment that while failure was quickly commented upon, achievement and success were not similarly acknowledged. This latter point is taken up by Gray (1979) when he suggests, 'Teachers need to feel successful and yet there are few occasions when they receive the affirming strokes they need.' He continues, 'For too long it has been assumed that only the intellects of teachers require development and many have become emotionally undernourished as a consequence.' His recommendation that staff counselling should be an integral part of college activity was echoed by the unit in its presentation to Management when considering a range of supportive strategies for the individual.

The unit presented a synthesis of its own findings and those of relevant research for the consideration of the principalship. Its summary of needs and responses, here presented only in outline, was accompanied by some sixty or seventy recommendations for action in the immediate, mid, and long term.

The Need			A Possible Response
1	For information; explanation; interpretation	to reduce feelings of bewilderment or ignorance	More sensitive communication systems with particular attention to feedback
2	For consultation; involvement	to reduce feelings of isolation and helplessness	Schemes for participation in decision making
3	For role clarification; criteria for performance	to reduce feelings of confusion and uncertainty	Task analysis, task allocation and training opportunities

4	For organization; planning	to reduce feelings of disorientation and harrassment	Communication of College Plan and departmental objective. Time management strategies
5	For credibility; job pride	to reduce feelings of failure and inadequacy	Training and development opportunities. Appraisal procedures
6	For recognition; reward	to reduce feelings of isolation and lack of worth	Regular sectional meetings. Personal job enhancement programmes

Thus the first stage of the stress initiative was concluded. It showed an acceptance by the principalship of the need to appraise the health of the institution by consultation at all levels and to take actions based not merely on organizational needs as perceived from the top, but much more strongly on needs voiced by staff across the college in both teaching and administration; it would seem to approach the partnership model of staff development advocated by Yorke (1977), though as yet its success in this respect has not been fully evaluated. Within six months the following developments were under way in the college arising from the recommendations accepted by Management.

1 A programme of annual personal development consultations between all staff and their heads of department, as described more fully by Shears (1982b).
2 A staff development programme for heads of department as the key figures in mediating both change and constraint to their staff.
3 A series of 'tea parties' at which all staff eventually would have the opportunity to seek information from and raise issues with the principalship.
4 Continued encouragement of staff to seek qualified teacher status, and the allocation of scarce resources to this.
5 Short periods of industrial placement for updating the skills and knowledge base of teaching staff.
6 The establishment of teaching methods groups.
7 The establishment of support groups for staff involved in student counselling (Britain and Shears 1981; Shears 1981).
8 The elaboration of the role of both unit personnel and the team of departmental staff development representatives in developing staff counselling across the college.
9 The metamorphosis of one of the unit's two posts into that of professional tutor with a remit to support new staff through an enhanced induction programme, including a short course in basic teaching skills, and to offer support to staff undertaking teacher certification courses.
10 Elaboration of the function of the college news sheet to provide fuller communication of management/local authority decisions and to acknowledge success and achievement among staff and students.
11 The restructuring of the Staff Development Committee to reflect departmental concerns more closely and to encourage heads of department to commit

resources to programmes for staff development which they would in future work out in consultation with their staff.

12 The reversion of the Staff Development Unit to a reactive role mainly concerned with facilitating the programme of activities required by heads of department.

13 Extensive planning of development programmes for those staff needing to change their teaching methods and styles of relationship to meet a changing student population.

A formal evaluation of the effectiveness of the stress initiative has not yet been carried out. Certainly it resulted in a good deal of activity. There is no doubt that it contributed to an extensive reappraisal of the internal dynamic of the college and would seem fully to exemplify a response based on foresight, firmness and compassion, underpinned by extensive supporting documentation either from research or relevant literature.

The context of the initiative bears re-emphasis, in that the college was at this time under pressure to diversity its courses, to take in new categories of student, to carry out the necessary training and retraining of staff that this implied, all at a rapid pace and in a period of recession. Tolley (1979) finds the requirements on colleges 'to do more and better with the same or less' an exciting challenge producing its own opportunities. Many staff would react to this with panic on the one hand and on the other a demand for support structures, development opportunities and a commitment by the organization to adapt its structures and strictures to meet the needs of the individual teacher and administrator. The stress initiative in some measure assisted in the alleviation of the first response and the articulation of the second.

The unit can also be seen to have fulfilled some of the functions described by Warren Piper (1975) in both acting as a catalyst (or maybe synergist, since it was, itself, changed in the process!) and in contributing to change in the climate of the institution; in this case 'putting stress on the agenda' so that its effects could be examined openly and a genuine commitment to work for their better management could follow. This could be seen, in the context of recession, as an institution making the best use of its most valuable resource, the staff themselves.

REFERENCES

Britain, N. and Shears, P.A. (1981) Guidance in further education — a progress report *Further Education Network Newsletter* 5, 11-12

Cooper, C.L. and Marshall, J. (1978) *Understanding Executive Stress* London: Macmillan

Cox, T. (1978) *Stress* London: Macmillan

Edmands, U. (1980) *A Survey of the Internal Communication Systems in Newcastle College of Arts and Technology: a preliminary study* Unpublished research made available to the College Principal

Ferguson, C.T. (1980) Stress *Coombe Lodge Working Paper* Information Bank No. 1559

Gray, H.L. (1979) Staff counselling in education *Journal of Further and Higher Education* 3 (1) 75-81

Kahn, R.L. et al. (1964) *Organizational Stress* New York: Wiley

Lazarus, R.S. (1966) *Psychological Stress and the Coping Process* New York: McGraw-Hill

Owen, R.E. (1979) The changing rôle of the lecturer in further education *National Association of Staff Development Journal* 1, 3-9

Pearse, R. (1978) The manager in the mirror *Behavioural Sciences Newsletter Special Report*

Selye, H. (1974) *Stress Without Distress* Philadelphia: J.B. Lippincott

Shears, P.A. (1981) Support groups for staff involved in counselling in a city F.E. college *Further Education Network Newsletter* 3, 6-7

Shears, P.A. (1982a) Someone give me an answer: a consideration of the aims and purposes of F.E. *Liberal Education* Autumn 1982

Shears, P.A. (1982b) Developing a system of appraisal of performance within a college of non advanced further education *Evaluation Newsletter* 6 (1) 21-30

Spielberger, C. (1979) *Understanding Stress and Anxiety* London: Harper & Row

Toffler, A. (1970) *Future Shock* New York: Random House

Tolley, G. (1979) Staff development in a rapidly changing situation *National Association of Staff Development Journal* 1, 21-27

Turner, C. (1975) Managing change *Coombe Lodge Report* 8 (4)

Turner, C. (1977) Organizing educational institutions as anarchies *The Journal of the British Educational Society* 5 (2) 6-11

Warren Piper, D. (1975) The longer reach *Issues in Staff Development* UTMU; p. 1-19

Yorke, D.M. (1976) Staff development: an essay in ambiguity? *Proceedings of the conference 'Strategies for Staff Development'* Manchester Polytechnic, p. 10-20 (mimeo)

Yorke, D.M. (1977) The development of staff and their counselling *Coombe Lodge Information Bank* No. 1215

12 STAFF DEVELOPMENT AND INNOVATION THEORY

Desmond Rutherford and Haydn Mathias   University of Birmingham and University of Southampton

Staff development came in on the flood-tide of the Robbins expansion of higher education but now seems in danger of being swept out on the ebb of recession. According to Becher and Kogan (1980), it was a movement, like educational technology and student counselling, 'which has come and gone, leaving behind an identifiable residue but somehow failing to transform the status quo' (p. 129). They explain staff development's lack of impact in terms of an innovation which originated from interest groups outside rather than within institutions, and which emphasized change in the operational mode (ie affecting practice) rather than in the normative mode (ie affecting basic values and norms).

However, the residue Becher and Kogan refer to is not insignificant and retains a potential for innovation in a climate of recession. Matheson (1981) in his detailed account of the growth of staff development in British universities notes that, whereas in 1972-73 nearly all staff development activities were organized by academics on a voluntary basis, by 1979-80 there were individuals in thirty-three universities with specific responsibilities for staff development. Of these thirty-three 'staff developers', eleven were full-time appointments, seven part-time appointments and fifteen undertook this responsibility as part of their other academic duties.

If this significant residue of staff developers is to have an influence in universities within a climate of recession, it needs not only to identify important areas for change, but also to understand the nature and process of change. Therefore, staff development is considered here within an innovation and change perspective. Through the application of a particular model of innovation to two staff development initiatives in two universities, it aims to demonstrate one way in which staff development may be conceptualized as a basis for guiding and evaluating decisions and actions.

THE CONTEXT OF STAFF DEVELOPMENT
Universities are complex institutions. Hewton (1979a, 1982) has suggested that they are characterized by an organizational system based on subject departments; a value system which stresses the autonomy of both individual academics and departments; a decision-making system which relies on a complex committee structure to encourage debate and dissent but one in which the actual decision-making process is obscure; and a covert power system which is largely controlled by heads of departments.

This context presents several problems for staff development. At the institutional level, central policy is likely to be difficult to implement since the centres of power are so diffuse. Hogan (1980) argued that it is no longer possible to regard complex organizations as 'purposive systems' since both individuals and groups often have conflicting priorities and hence are unable to reach consensus over common goals. This has become increasingly evident in universities' attempts to formulate policy in a time of recession. Although there is a tendency towards an increased degree of centralization, there are also signs of an increased differentiation in the influence over policy which different departments are able to exert by virtue of their relative success in attracting research funds and students (Davies and Morgan 1982). Staff development policies may, therefore, depend on identifying and influencing the 'strong' departments and the powerful 'barons' at their head.

Influencing the key departments, and hence the academics, may not be sufficient, however, if staff development is not incorporated into those departments' normative values. There may be temporary interest and changes in practice but these are likely to fade as the external catalyst is withdrawn and as individual academics' priorities are reassessed. For as Hewton (1982) argued, the uncertainty created by autonomy not only affects the traditional academic balancing of demands among teaching, research, administrative and external commitments, but also the balance between work and leisure. In order to cope with autonomy, the acceptable compromise reached by an academic in these areas becomes a stabilizing factor and a means of coping with an open situation. Finding time for educational development at an individual level may mean unacceptable sacrifices unless there are fundamental shifts in values and organizational arrangements at a departmental level.

PERSPECTIVES ON STAFF DEVELOPMENT

Staff development activities in universities have predominantly been concerned with the improvement of teaching. There are strong historical reasons for this (Matheson 1981) but there have also been institutional barriers to expansion into other areas, such as research, promotion and staff development leave. In their review of the growth of staff development policies in universities and polytechnics, Greenaway and Harding (1978) noted that different institutional committees usually had traditional responsibility for these different areas. Broadening the concept of staff development to include all aspects of the individual's development can therefore be extremely difficult, given established and vested interests in areas other than teaching, and may create considerable tension between the institution's expectations and a staff developer's aspirations.

Although scope for expansion into other areas of staff development may be limited, there may be opportunities for modest co-ordination among the various interest groups. However, this can present the staff developer with another dilemma. Areas such as salaries and promotion are extremely sensitive and any association that a staff developer forms with such areas may well adversely affect the relationship he has with academics. The staff developer may not only be seen as undeservedly influential by fellow academics, but also as operating in an evaluative rather than in a facilitative mode in his relationships with his colleagues.

Given that the staff developer is likely to be primarily concerned with educational development, his professional relationship with academics may be characterized in a number of ways. He may regard himself as an expert where he either responds to a problem with a solution or solutions, or offers to diagnose the precise nature of the problem and then to prescribe a solution. He may regard himself as a counsellor, where the emphasis is on helping academics to explore the nature of their own teaching problems and how they might deal with them once identified. He may regard himself as a consultant emphasizing the solution of an immediate problem — a 'product' orientation — or the development of the personal and professional skills of the academic involved — a 'process' orientation. Finally, he may regard himself as a fellow colleague working with the academic jointly on some problem. Boud and McDonald (1981) clarify these roles and argue that, when working with individual academics, the staff developer needs to draw upon each of these traditions and adopt an eclectic approach. However, these roles represent markedly different philosophies and it is likely that a staff developer will lean more heavily on one than on the others.

Not only is the contribution that a staff developer might make heavily dependent on his conceptualization of his role, but also on the organizational support that the institution provides. Rutherford (1983) has outlined the advantages and disadvantages of four different approaches: the University Committee (no full or part-time staff developer); the Independent Unit (the staff developer is given fairly wide terms of reference and is expected to exercise his responsibilities as he sees fit); the Semi-independent Unit (the staff developer works closely with a committee of academic staff who see their primary role as one of advising and supporting him); the Working Group (activities are implemented by small groups of academic staff drawn from a university committee who are supported by a staff developer).

INSIGHTS FROM THEORIES OF INNOVATION

Staff development is about change. Theories of innovation and change have offered insights into how staff development might be effectively brought about both in terms of policy implementation and practical impact. Chin and Benne's (1976) three strategies of planned change (power-coercive, rational-empirical and normative-re-educative) have been applied to the areas of staff development and educational development by several authors (eg Hewton 1979b and Hawkridge 1979) and have gone some way towards identifying how different outcomes are likely to be achieved and through which kinds of strategies and processes. However, these strategies are fairly general and thereby limited when it comes to examining the effectiveness of particular policies and procedures at a detailed level.

Change is a political and often a conflict-ridden process. It takes place in institutional settings which have their own unique histories, value systems and traditions, organizational and power structures, and social contexts which interact with the process of change. If the staff developer is to facilitate educational change he needs to take account of the response to change within the complex context of the institutional setting. Berg and Ostergren (1977, 1979) derived a model of innovation which goes some way to recognizing the political and social context of change and which may offer the staff developer an adequate perspective through which to evaluate and guide his activities (see for example Rutherford 1982). Although developed through a study of curriculum innovation in Swedish higher education, the model seems readily transferable to staff development in the United Kingdom.

Berg and Ostergren argue that individual behaviours are strongly influenced by the particular interest groups to which they belong. Therefore they suggest that the various groups — both social and organizational — which make up the institutional system need to be identified and their inter-relationships explored. Through their analysis of several innovations they derived four decisive factors which they argued enabled them to explain why some innovations were successful and why others failed. The four factors are: gain/loss (the perceived advantages and disadvantages for groups and individuals, particularly in the areas of security/stability and personal satisfaction/self-realization as a consequence of the innovation); ownership (the quality of feeling that groups and individuals experience because of their involvement in the creation and introduction of the innovation and hence the commitment to its success); leadership (ie the influence of different kinds of leaders on the process of the innovation, eg primary, secondary, formal and opposition leaders); and power (eg the exercise or the threat of the exercise of power to implement, sustain and institutionalize the innovation).

To summarize, the model predicts that an innovation is likely to be successful if there are clear gains and few losses to be made, a strong sense of ownership, effective leadership, and a sensitive and timely exercise of power to secure the innovation. Innovation processes are, however, dynamic so that the characteristics of gains and losses, ownership, leadership and power may differ and may exert variable influences over the passage of time. We shall now consider the application of Berg and Ostergren's model in the analysis of two staff development activities in two universities — Birmingham and Southampton. If this theoretical perspective offers useful insights then the four decisive factors may provide the basis of a practical 'theory of action' for staff developers.

THE CASE STUDIES
Both the University of Birmingham and the University of Southampton have appointed full-time staff developers. Birmingham is a large and established university with over 1,000 academic staff and 8,500 students. The staff developer is known as the Organizing Tutor for the Advisory Service on Teaching Methods and although based in the Faculty of Education is responsible to the university's Educational Development Advisory Committee. Southampton is a medium-sized university with some 750 academic staff and 6,000 students. The staff developer is in the Department of Teaching Media which has an academic role in the Faculty of Educational Studies as well as an educational media production and support role in the university. Staff development activities are initiated in collaboration with an inter-faculty working party.

At Birmingham the 'working group' approach (Rutherford 1983) has proved the most satisfactory way of organizing staff development, with the staff developer taking on the role of the 'fellow colleague'. In contrast, organizational arrangements at Southampton are more akin to the 'semi-independent unit', with the staff developer taking on a mixture of 'consultant' and 'fellow colleague' roles. Nevertheless, staff development initiatives appear to follow a rather similar pattern in each institution: induction/initial training courses for new staff; formal·in-service activities (eg workshops, seminars, etc.) for established staff; information and resource services (eg occasional publications, newsletters, video-recording); opportunities for the evaluation of courses and teaching; consultancy and collaboration with individuals and departments on specific projects; grants to staff to improve their own courses or to attend occasional conferences/workshops elsewhere. This common core of activities belies differences in emphasis in certain areas of activity between both institutions. We shall take one recent but different development in each institution as a basis for our case studies and analyse and evaluate them in terms of Berg and Ostergren's model.

Case 1: Information and Resources — a Newsletter (Birmingham)
For the last five years a newsletter — *Teaching News* — has been published once a term by the Educational Development Advisory Committee at the University of Birmingham. During this period over 150 articles have been published with the great majority of these having been written by academics at Birmingham. *Teaching News* is circulated to all academic staff in the university and to an increasing number of interested colleagues (currently about 600) in other institutions. The newsletter is produced by a small working group drawn from the committee (Rutherford 1982) which consists of a senior editor, a junior editor and an executive editor (the staff developer). To date, a total of seven academics have been involved as

either senior of junior editor.

Can Berg and Ostergren's theory provide some explanation of the factors that have determined the success of this particular innovation? First of all, a number of interested groups can be identified: the editors; the committee; the authors; the readers (both in the university and outside). Of these, the editorial group is perhaps the most important: their ownership is direct and total and consequently commitment is high. There are substantial gains to be made particularly in the areas of personal satisfaction/self-realization through being involved in a successful innovation. Potential losses could arise if the amount of time and energy demanded became excessive but this is minimized by the rotation of editors and the support of the staff developer. The leadership offered by the senior editor is obviously of crucial importance: first, he has the primary responsibility for developing a distinctive editorial policy, which focuses on current concerns, and for soliciting contributions; secondly, he has to act as an advocate for the newsletter at meetings of the committee and informally to members of the University.

The committee itself supports *Teaching News* but, in accordance with the accepted traditions of academic autonomy, tends not to interfere in matters of day-to-day editorial policy and so experiences a degree of indirect ownership. However, wider issues of policy are debated (e.g. the relatively high costs) and it is recognized that the power to determine the future of the newsletter does rest with the committee. Furthermore, the policy of appointing senior and junior editors was agreed by the committee and it is the chairman who invites (or cajoles) members to act as editors (one of his most important leadership functions).

Perhaps the most welcome outcome of the years of publication is the large number of academics from Birmingham (well over 100) who have contributed to *Teaching News*. Although unsolicited articles have never been numerous, most colleagues have been willing to write when asked (and given enough time!). It is a substantial challenge having to write an article for one's colleagues describing, for example, an innovation in a course or in a method of teaching. And the resultant gains involved in personal satisfaction are possibly quite considerable. Unfortunately, it is extremely rare for university teachers to be explicit about such matters. Editorial control — censorship is too harsh a description — has sometimes necessitated extensive re-writing of articles to ensure that authors are not 'harmed' by their publication (ie eliminating losses). This wide authorship has increased the degree of direct but partial ownership in *Teaching News* among academics at Birmingham and may be an important factor in establishing its reputation and ensuring its survival.

Gains for the wider readership in the university are difficult to determine without extensive research. Hopefully, there may be a greatly increased knowledge and awareness of issues relating to teaching and learning and the continued publication of *Teaching News* is perhaps an obvious sign of the university's concern for such matters. In addition, certain rather provocative issues (eg alternative prospectus, library cuts, affirmative action) which may not have been given the attention they deserved have been fully debated. *Teaching News* is one of the most successful innovations in staff development at the University of Birmingham and it appears that the theoretical perspective which Berg and Ostergren have developed (ie the analysis of how the four decisive factors — gain/loss, ownership, leadership and power relate to the various interest groups) provides considerable insight into the reasons for that success.

Case 2: Local Staff Development (*Southampton*)
This case study describes a local initiative in an engineering department which had a history of interest in educational development. About two years ago negotiations with senior academics in the department resulted in a proposal whereby a number of lecturers would be invited to have one of their lectures observed and video-recorded by the staff developer as a basis for providing feedback on their lecturing. The longer-term aim was to establish an acceptable means whereby lecturers could regularly monitor and review their own teaching. A departmental request for volunteers produced four willing lecturers whom the staff developer was invited to contact. Each of the four lecturers was observed and video-recorded. Two lecturers viewed and discussed their recorded lectures with the staff developer individually. However, the other two agreed to a joint viewing session and felt that this had been valuable in terms of the quality of feedback they had obtained.

This activity received further support in the following year. The department assigned a young lecturer as a liaison person to help organize another round of video recordings. This time three lecturers agreed to be observed and recorded and although each was seen individually to view and discuss his lecture, two agreed to allow the video recordings to be shown to other colleagues. A seminar was organized by the staff developer and the departmental liaison person which reviewed and evaluated the lecture feedback activity, discussed case studies (including the viewing of excerpts of two of the video-recorded lectures) and drew out common problems. All seven lecturers took part in the seminar, together with as many other departmental colleagues. As a result, it was agreed that at least one departmental meeting a term should specifically involve lecturers in the evaluation activity and discuss aspects of the feedback gained.

How successful was this innovation? Analysis in terms of Berg and Ostergren's four decisive factors provides clues to the answer to this question. For the lecturer involved in the innovation, the gains were largely intrinsic and mainly in terms of opportunities to develop and receive reassurance on his teaching. In terms of losses, there were: the additional time required not only in involvement in the innovation, but also in changing practice, if necessary; for some, the threat to existing and familiar practice and their self-esteem; and for some again, the lack of formal recognition or rewards for their participation.

The staff developer had promoted the idea of departmental ownership of the innovation. However, until it could be established as a group-based activity, there was a tendency for lecturers to view it as an individual service. The departmental seminar formed the basis for the development of a group who could take over responsibility for the innovation. Thus, the innovation was about to enter a crucial phase where the staff developer had to work in conjunction with the departmental liaison person to ensure that such a group was established and effect the complete transfer of ownership to the department.

Although the staff developer played a primary leadership role, he felt that this would be more effective if it were perceived to be emanating not from an 'outsider' but from inside the department. Thus he relied on key senior academics and the departmental liaison person to take on the role. However, the effectiveness of their leadership depended not only on their commitment to the innovation, but also on the time they were willing to spend on it. Several academics who had been involved in the innovation could be identified as secondary leaders and could be called upon to support it. No significant opposition leaders had been identified but this was probably because the innovation was still at an informal stage of development and had not effectively threatened vested interests.

The support of senior academics exerted an element of power which launched the innovation. However, the form of this power was persuasive and, although influential, could not in itself secure the innovation. Effective power could only be exercised by mutual consent through the formal departmental meeting. Thus a strategy needed to be developed to introduce the innovation into the department's formal decision-making machinery.

In summary, the analysis reveals that the innovation is at an early stage of development and that more needs to be done to secure its implementation. The gains for participants need to be marginally more extrinsic; ownership of the innovation needs to be transferred more completely to the department; the departmental primary leaders need to maintain its impetus; and the formal approval of the department's main decision-making body needs to be gained in order to establish a secure power base. At this stage, therefore, the staff developer has an even more important role to play in facilitating the innovation and promoting its merits in a time of recession where the quality of teaching can very easily become an early casualty.

FUTURE PROSPECTS

Our brief analyses of two staff development initiatives using a much simplified version of Berg and Ostergren's model have illustrated one useful means of evaluating and managing these and other kinds of staff development activities. The model provides a level of conceptualization which is economic yet sufficiently flexible to respond to the characteristics of different situations. Furthermore, it roots the process of change firmly in the social, political and institutional setting in which it takes place. It seems to us that if the staff developer is to continue as a catalyst for innovation rather than become a casualty of recession, then he must develop a greater understanding of the factors which facilitate and inhibit change and development in his own institutional setting. A model of innovation and change such as Berg and Ostergren's should provide him with a way of evaluating his present activities and even help to decide on future priorities in a climate of recession.

However, a model of innovation in itself will not predict the future prospects for staff development. Staff developers will need to examine the likely consequences of recession for their own roles. The resources and the priority that have been previously accorded to training and development programmes for new academic staff will inevitably decrease as the number of appointees fall. Yet the need to provide training for new lecturers — particularly those on probation — is one of the few policies in staff development that senates have been able to approve. If this activity were to cease, the survival of staff development units would become much more problematic. Staff developers will have to find ways of retaining and developing this one source of legitimizing power, for in the absence of this decisive factor (Berg and Ostergren) staff development will be in an extremely weak position within universities.

For experienced staff, consolidation rather than innovation may well be the watchword. The increased pressure of work may result in even fewer members of staff seeking to develop radically new methods of teaching; staff developers will need to give a high priority to supporting and encouraging those few who continue to innovate. As prospects for promotion diminish academics may seek greater satisfaction in their present jobs rather than seek radical changes in their practices. The staff developer obviously has a role in this area in improving practice. It may even provide a welcome opportunity for him to consolidate his own 'training' skills in a relatively few basic teaching methods where there is currently a profusion of strategies and materials.

However, consolidation rather than innovation through recession is effective only in the short term, for in a fast changing world such a conservative policy could leave universities at a severe disadvantage. Recession has given the university system a sharp jolt which has unfrozen a good deal of conventional practice. If the staff developer does not take the opportunity to influence a changing situation, he will find himself frozen out as the system sets into a different pattern.

REFERENCES

Becher, T. and Kogan, M. (1980) *Process and Structure in Higher Education* London: Heinemann

Berg, B. and Ostergren, B. (1977) *Innovations and Innovation Processes in Higher Education* Stockholm: National Board of Universities and Colleges

Berg, B. and Ostergren, B. (1979) Innovation processes in higher education *Studies in Higher Education* 4, 261-268

Boud, D. and McDonald, R. (1981) *Educational Development Through Consultancy* Guildford: Society for Research into Higher Education

Chin, R. and Benne, K.D. (1976) General strategies for effecting change in human systems. In Bennis, W.G., Benne, K.D., Chin, R. and Corey, K.E. (Editors) *The Planning of Change* London: Holt, Rinehart and Winston (Third edition)

Davies, J.L. and Morgan, A.W. (1982) The politics of institutional change. In Wagner, L. (Editor) *Agenda for Institutional Change in Higher Education* Guildford: Society for Research into Higher Education

Greenaway, H. and Harding, A.G. (1978) *The Growth of Policies for Staff Development* Guildford: Society for Research into Higher Education

Hawkridge, D. (1979) Persuading the dons? *British Journal of Educational Technology* 10 (3) 164 - 174

Hewton, E. (1979a) A strategy for promoting curriculum development in universities *Studies in Higher Education* 4, 67 - 75

Hewton, E. (1979b) Towards a definition of staff development *Impetus* 11, 1 - 8

Hewton, E. (1982) *Rethinking Educational Change* Guildford: Society for Research into Higher Education

Hogan, D.F. (1980) New directions in the study of innovation *Royal Air Force Education Bulletin* 18, 127 - 134

Matheson, C.C. (1981) *Staff Development Matters* Norwich: Co-ordinating Committee for the Training of University Teachers

Rutherford, D. (1982) Developing university teaching: a strategy for revitalization *Higher Education* 11, 177 - 191

Rutherford, D. (1983) An analysis of four institutional strategies for staff development *British Journal of Educational Technology* 14, 4 - 13

13 STUDENT SELF-ASSESSMENT

David Boud and Jacqueline Lublin   University of Sydney and University of New South Wales

In terms of the effective management of resources in education, students themselves are constantly overlooked and consequently under-utilized. In 1970, MacKenzie, Eraut and Jones drew attention to the potential for the use of students. However, there have been few attempts to follow up their suggestions in higher education. Since the economic climate in tertiary institutions has changed greatly in the last twelve years, it may be profitable to return to the question of the use of students in teaching roles to see if there is scope for improving the quality of education within existing resource levels. The general area of students as teachers was well covered in Cornwall's (1979) excellent monograph on peer assisted learning. Here we focus on the use of students as assessors.

THE MEANING OF SELF-ASSESSMENT
In this context we use the word assessment to mean determining the extent of student achievement. Any assessment process has two fundamental aspects: the determining of the criteria to be used as a yardstick to measure, or judge, the extent and quality of learning; and the application of these criteria to students' work. Traditionally, it has been taken for granted that staff alone should set the learning goals and then choose and apply the criteria to evaluate whether these have been achieved. We refer to this as unilateral assessment (Heron 1981).

We can identify at least two situations in which students can take an active role in the process by which they are assessed: where criteria are determined by staff but applied by students to themselves; and where criteria are both determined and applied by students. Both of these have been called self-assessment, but the former (self-marking) is clearly a more limited case of the latter. A third situation might be mentioned in passing, which is one where students set the learning goals themselves and also determine and apply criteria. This is more commonly seen in non-traditional programmes (Berte 1975) or adult education courses (Knowles 1975).

THE VALUE OF SELF-ASSESSMENT
Although informal self-assessment is probably a prerequisite for all forms of learning, at present their are few or no opportunities in most courses for students to develop formally their skills of self-appraisal. We believe that it is important that students should develop this capacity for several reasons. First, the ability to assess oneself and one's performance realistically is an essential component of competent professional practice. Also, self-assessment is a necessary component of independent or autonomous thinking and must be fostered if courses aspire to the development of critical thinking in students. If students are only exposed to unilateral assessments by their teachers and are not placed in situations where they must make decisions about their own work, they cannot be expected to develop these higher level abilities which are alleged to be the hallmark of a higher education. Indeed, it could be said that as one of the main aims of higher education is to encourage individual responsibility in learning, one of the complementary aims must be to encourage individual responsibility in assessment, ie that students should move from a position

of dependence in assessment to a position of independence where they can make their own realistic estimates of the nature and extent of their learning. Self-assessment does not, however, imply that students set criteria or make judgements in isolation from others. What characterizes self-assessment is that students ultimately make decisions on criteria and performance which may of course be informed by statements from teachers, peers, professional practitioners and the appropriate literature.

THE PROBLEMS OF SELF-ASSESSMENT

Although the encouragement of self-assessment can clearly be justified in terms of the supposed goals of higher education, its adoption may pose problems for both staff and students. The main issue concerns the overwhelming influence of the formal assessment system and the expectations which this engenders. Students expect to be evaluated by others. They have been conditioned not to trust their own judgements and have been placed in a situation of dependency in which they respond to the requirements of the formal assessment system, often placing more emphasis on this than on their own learning needs and on developing their own standards of competence. Furthermore, assessment is one of the central features of the teacher's role in higher education and is now almost the only element for the control of students which remains exclusively in the hands of academic staff. It requires staff to take a risk, albeit small, if they are to share with students any element of what has been their traditional prerogative. Thus both staff and students may reveal a very understandable reluctance to take the risk of moving away from traditional positions of power and powerlessness.

Another matter which clouds the issue of self-assessment is the large scale move in recent years towards what is known as continuous assessment. Students now usually expect all work they produce to be graded and to contribute in some way to their final assessment. The notion of working to learn has been displaced by the notion of working for grades. One of the most frequently heard justifications for continuous assessment is that it provides feedback to students on their progress. However, when such feedback also carries a mark counting towards a final assessment it is no longer purely diagnostic, ie it is both formative and summative. Miller (1976) showed the educational paradox involved in this situation when he argued that assessment for diagnostic feedback should be kept separate from assessment for marks or certification. This has important implications for self-assessment. If students are to be given opportunities to practise self-assessment, should this be simply for diagnostic feedback purposes or should it also lead to formal grades. An answer to this question is of crucial importance if students are to be encouraged to change their traditional attitudes and to accept some responsibility for assessment. Crudely, what extrinsic incentive is there to do so, if their evaluations are never allowed to contribute to their final marks? If, however, self-assessments are to be formally recognized, can these be reconciled with society's need for accreditation by those designated competent to judge?

INTRODUCING SELF-ASSESSMENT

In light of the above, we have been exploring areas where self-assessment activities might be introduced, and in some subjects looking at the extent to which students do in fact seem able to make responsible assessments of their own performance. There seem to be many activities which would help students to make judgements about themselves from their earliest days. These include giving feedback to peers on their work; making judgements of the quality of their own work and that of others in the light of given criteria, and, potentially, in areas in which they had demonstrated their own competence; awarding grades to themselves and others. Educationally, what is of importance is that students develop an increasingly sophisticated understanding of the area which they are studying, that they have an appreciation of appropriate criteria which they can apply to the topic, and that they are capable of applying these criteria to their own work. We believe that the judgement of their peers as well as the judgement of staff is important in helping students to be realistic about their own work. These activities may well demand a new role for staff and for students, and it may place an additional responsibility on students, which they might resist initially. It may also provide a challenge to staff who will need to moderate the assessments of students rather than always being the prime assessors.

Another constraint is of course that of resources. If the introduction of self-assessment activities is to be acceptable, then it must not make demands on present budgets; indeed, if possible it should lead to economies of staff time. It is important to point out that with one exception the main rationale for all the examples which follow was an improved quality of experience for the students who took part. We believe, however, that our results do point towards areas where savings can be made which will allow the more effective deployment of the most expensive resource of all, staff time.

STUDIES IN SELF-ASSESSMENT

In investigating the possibilities for self-assessment and the perceived congruence of student judgements with those of staff we looked at the abilities of more junior undergraduates to apply given criteria to their own work, and the abilities of senior or final year undergraduates both to develop criteria and to apply these to their own work. One investigation (Lublin 1980) asked students in a materials engineering course at the New South Wales Institute of Technology (half way through a four-year engineering course) to estimate their likely performance on all assessable work in the one semester subject. This comprised three written reports, two open-book classroom exams and a final exam. It was found that the majority of students were quite reasonably able to estimate their performance. One issue in this case was the sheer number of assessable tasks imposed on students (and marking workload on staff). If this lecturer taught two classes in this subject during a semester with a class size of twenty-five, then he would be marking 300 reports, 200 class exams and fifty final exams. One implication for practice was that students themselves might take over the marking tasks of the ongoing tests, if they could be made diagnostic and not mark-bearing.

A second study went much further in involving the student as an active and judging participant in an assessment process which counted for final marks (Boud and Holmes 1981). This occurred in a course on electronic circuits at the University of New South Wales (in the third year of a four-year engineering course): as an alternative to the normal marking procedure for a mid-term examination, it was decided to involve students as markers and to provide them with model answers to which they could compare the solutions in completed examination papers and allocate marks. In the first class following the examination, students were randomly allocated the unnamed paper of one other student in the class (of over one hundred students). This they marked in their own time following the model answers and marking schedule. They were required to indicate in detail on a marking sheet exactly where the other student had deviated from the model solutions and to award a score for each section on a scale provided. They returned the papers and marking sheets the following week and received their own examination script. They then applied the same procedure to their own paper without knowing the marks already awarded. The self and peer marks for the examination were then compared. If the percentage marks were within 10% of each other the student was awarded the self-mark. If there was a greater than 10% discrepancy, the paper was re-marked by a staff member. In addition, other papers were sampled at random to discourage mark-fixing. A procedure for administering this scheme was evolved over four successive courses in the same subject to minimize staff time, to ensure equitable distribution of papers, and to minimize collusion in mark-fixing. Student response was good and staff reported that there was a considerable saving in marking time, even allowing for the increase in time in preparing model answers and organizing the movement of papers. The larger the number of students in the class, the greater the saving.

A more sophisticated approach to the provision of feedback was taken in another context. In final-year courses, and particularly in project work, it might be expected that students will have a reasonable view of the criteria which should apply to their own work. However, they may not have had enough experience to develop these and apply them in an objective way. They need alternative viewpoints from which to examine their own work. These can be provided by staff, but it is difficult for students not to feel obliged to conform to staff views when staff are the ultimate assessors. In this case peers are a useful source of ideas and opinions.

Such an approach was adopted in a final-year design subject in a landscape architecture degree course at the University of New South Wales. A few weeks after receiving a design brief students were invited individually to determine the criteria which they considered should be applied to the outcomes of the design project. These included both general considerations of good design and factors which are unique to the particular problem which had been set. When the projects were complete, the students met for a session in which they each had the opportunity of receiving feedback from their peers on their own design. Following this, students completed a self-assessment of their own project in the light of their original criteria, suitably modified in the light of their own experience and that of the feedback from their peers. In this case the outcomes did not form part of the formal assessment system, but students appreciated the opportunity for feedback on their work.

Another two investigations at the New South Wales Institute of Technology are currently examining the extent to which final-year undergraduates in professional faculties are able to be realistic assessors of their own abilities. In both faculties, mechanical engineering and architecture, there is a final extended project which represents the student's last experience of undergraduate requirements and attempts a close simulation of the requirements of professional practice. These projects are intended to draw together the disparate strands of undergraduate learning into an integrated approach to a real-life professional problem. In neither case are the criteria for judging the projects spelled out by staff: in mechanical engineering the project in report form was examined by two independent assessors, while in architecture the project in graphic and three-dimensional form was assessed by a jury. In these investigations it has been decided to invite students to engage in a full self-assessment, ie to choose criteria, weight them, then apply them. This self-assessment will be compared with the assessment made by staff. Our hunch, also supported by some others' evidence (Keefer 1971; Stanton 1978) is that students at this level will have a fairly accurate appreciation of their abilities.

In a mechanical engineering design course at the University of New South Wales it was decided to include a weighting for self-assessment in the formal examination system, to encourage students to treat it seriously. This involved staff awarding an additional mark worth up to 4% to students who gave a perceptive and accurate self-appraisal of their own work, independent of the mark awarded for the work itself. It appears that a token weighting might influence students to take the process of self-assessment seriously. The need for students to be given the incentive of marks associated with self-assessment seems to vary depending on circumstances, as in the landscape architecture study this was never an issue. Once students have had the experience of a well-designed self-assessment scheme, which relates closely to the course, much of their resistance seems to disappear. However, if self-assessment demands a significantly higher work load, especially at the time of other assessment pressures, then resistance may remain.

IMPLICATIONS
All the preceding examples were introduced into existing courses without affecting the content and goals of the courses. They involved a minimal disruption of what would normally have occurred in the classes and in some cases did not involve any class time at all. On the other hand, they did provide students with additional feedback over and above that which they would normally have received; they required students to a greater or lesser extent to consider actively and apply criteria of competence appropriate to the subject; and they required closer attention than normal to be paid to the process of learning in the course and to organizational matters. They involved students taking rather more responsibility than may have been the case previously, but they did not require staff to forgo their basic responsibility for assessment.

These are a few examples which have occurred in our own institutions and we are aware of many others which have gone unheralded elsewhere. For example, nineteen examples were provided by participants in a workshop we conducted on this subject earlier in the year in Melbourne. While we do not pretend that these are having a significant impact on higher education, they do show what is possible.

Some elements of self-assessment have the potential for saving staff time. Perhaps the greatest saving could be in time spent on giving feedback to students and in marking routine work. While it would be undesirable to remove teachers completely from direct involvement in these activities there are many occasions on which students do not receive sufficient feedback and guidance on their work, or in which it is not necessary for the source of feedback to be the teachers themselves. This has been demonstrated in the Keller Plan approach to teaching (Boud, Bridge and Willoughby 1975). However, if staff marking time is to be saved, then there needs to be a greater investment of time in planning assessment activities, particularly when they are first introduced. One implication of this is that the savings may be greatest when large numbers of students are involved, or when the same course is offered on a number of occasions.

Another area where staff time may be saved could eventually emerge after a thorough investigation of the extent of correlation between staff assessment and student self-assessment in senior years. If the conditions under which tolerable correlations occur can be identified, then a form of contracting for marks by the student, with spot checks by staff and evaluative input by peers may well be a feasible procedure in some assessable areas. Some United States work on grade contracting pursues these ideas (Hassencahl 1979; O'Kane 1971; Popper and Thompson 1971; Taylor 1971). Such saving of staff time, however, is not likely to be significant at the institutional level. Rather, we see it as allowing a more effective deployment of available staff time in a way which will best enhance student learning, ie by freeing staff from some routine tasks and thus allowing them to direct time to the learning needs of groups or individuals. Indeed many of the educational benefits could be lost if zealous administrators tried to introduce self-assessment as a direct cost-cutting measure. Further considerable saving of staff marking time is available through various mechanical or electronic aids in some areas of assessment. These include cheap optical scanner machines (Evans 1978) or computer-based approaches (Osborne and Potter 1979) but such approaches could hardly be called self-assessment.

The introduction of any other than ad hoc forms of self-assessment is very new (Boud 1980). We do not underestimate the difficulties which have to be faced in introducing any innovation at the present time, but we have argued that there is a good case for self-assessment. Most importantly, it pursues important educational objectives and it complements other learning activities. It can also be introduced on a small scale by individual teachers within their own courses, and can fit within existing timetables. It may be very appropriate for diagnostic feedback, but the question of the extent to which students can take some responsibility for awarding themselves marks which count as formal grades is as yet unresolved. It is premature to judge its real potential on the basis of the limited available evidence, but there are sufficient indications to suggest its application on a trial basis in various ways in many subjects. Our own work is focusing at present on the development of a range of approaches to self-assessment in professionally orientated subjects such as engineering, law and architecture. The acceptance of self-assessment with increasing levels of enthusiasm suggests scope for more systematic and extensive applications.

REFERENCES

Berte, N.R. (Editor) (1975) *Individualizing Education through Contract Learning* Alabama: University of Alabama Press

Boud, D.J. (1980) Self and peer assessment in higher and continuing professional education: an annotated bibliography *Tertiary Education Research Centre, Occasional Publication No 16* Sydney: University of New South Wales

Boud, D.J., Bridge, W.A. and Willoughby, L. (1975) PSI Now: a review of progress and problems *British Journal of Educational Technology* 6, 15-34

Boud, D.J. and Holmes, W.H. (1981) Self and peer marking in an undergraduate engineering course *IEEE Transactions on Education* E-24(4) 267-274

Cornwall, M.G. (1979) *Students as Teachers: Peer Teaching in Higher Education* Cowo-Publicatie 7906-01, Amsterdam: Universiteit van Amsterdam

Evans, O.M. (1978) Separation of testing for feedback and assessment purposes in physiology *Policy, Process, Content and Research in Health Science Education* Sydney: Cumberland College of Health Sciences 2, 763-767

Hassencahl, F. (1979) Contract Grading in the Classroom *Improving College and University Teaching* 27 (1) 30-33

Heron, J. (1981) Assessment revisited. In Boud, D.J. (Editor) *Developing Student Autonomy in Learning* London: Kogan Page; 55-68

Keefer, K.E. (1971) Characteristics of students who make accurate and inaccurate self-predictions of college achievement *Journal of Educational* Research 64 (9) 401-404

Knowles, M.S. (1975) *Self-Directed Learning: a Guide for Learners and Teachers* New York: Association Press

Lublin, J. (1980) Student Self Assessment: a case study *Assessment in Higher Education* 5 (3) 264-272

MacKenzie, N., Eraut, M. and Jones, H. (1970) *Teaching and Learning: an introduction to new methods and resources in higher education* Paris: UNESCO/IAU

Miller, G.E. (1976) Continuous assessment *Medical Education* 10, 81-86

O'Kane, J.M. (1971) *Having Students do the Grading* Improving College and University Teaching 19, 331-332

Osborne, R.J. and Potter, C.J. (1979) Self-evaluation tests using interactive computer terminals *Assessment in Higher Education* 4 (3) 171-179

Popper, W.A. and Thompson, C.L. (1971) The effect of grade contracts on student performance *Journal of Educational Research* 64 (9) 420-424

Stanton, H.E. (1978) Self-grading as an assessment method *Improving College and University Teaching* 26 (4) 236-238

Taylor, H. (1971) Student reaction to the grade contract *Journal of Educational Research* 64 (7) 311-314

14 COST-EFFECTIVENESS IN LABORATORY TEACHING

Lewis Elton   University of Surrey

In a recent article, the then vice-chancellor of Brunel University said (Bragg 1980, p. 127):

> 'It will no doubt be argued that the difficulty (of maintaining standards in the face of decreasing resources) can be resolved by improving the efficiency of the university. ... Technically this is true, but taken in its widest sense quality must suffer unless there is an actual waste in the system. One would hope that most of this has been eliminated in the costs and squeezes of the last few years and if it is not it is unlikely to be corrected by central direction.'

The correctness of the last nine words is likely to be verified once the effects of the 1981-84 cuts in higher education have been evaluated, but the hope expressed in the first half of the last sentence is surely ingenuous. To eliminate waste, it may not even be always appropriate to reduce costs, but it is always necessary to increase effectiveness (Wagner 1982, Ch. 3) and the system of higher education, which is notorious for never having seriously evaluated its own operation, is most unlikely to be as cost-effective as it might be. I propose to illustrate this point in connection with the teaching of practical work in laboratories which, because it is labour intensive, time consuming, requires specialized teaching spaces and often expensive equipment, is likely to be among the more expensive operations in higher education. What I hope to show is that the cost-effectiveness of this operation, particularly in introductory laboratories, can be increased, not by central direction, but by detailed and informed work at the level of the individual department or even the individual teacher. I shall do this largely on the basis of work carried out by myself, my immediate colleagues and my research students over the past fifteen years, which has provided us with a systematic understanding of the relationships between the aims, methods, content and assessment of laboratory teaching.

Our starting point was the well-documented dissatisfaction which academic teachers, first in the United States and later also in Britain, expressed about the effectiveness of laboratory teaching as they knew it, and which did not seem to change over the years. For instance, the American Commission on College Physics (1972) stated that 'expressions of the general dissatisfaction of both students and faculty with the traditional introductory laboratory grew more and more noisy during the 1960s until it became a dereliction of duty not to focus some CCP attention on this part of physics teaching.' Yet six years later, the chairman of the International Commission on Physics Education was still saying (French 1978) that 'it is in this area (of laboratory work) that we tend to feel most strongly, and most often, that our students are having an educational experience falling far short of what we would wish them to have.' Similar statements from both sides of the Atlantic can readily be found in other branches of science and engineering (see for example Dearden 1979, Ch.1 and Watson 1980, Ch.2).

The persistence of this dissatisfaction in spite of an enormous effort to improve laboratory teaching during those years is likely to owe much to the fact that the effort was often misapplied, in that it concentrated on superficial innovations, mainly in order to keep pace with the development of the subject, and largely ignored the more profound changes of method which were needed in order to improve learning (Ogborn 1977). A simple statistic illustrates this (Elton 1975): the cumulative index of the American Journal of Physics for 1963-72 has twenty-two pages on 'Aids to physics teaching: hardware', eighteen pages on 'Aids to physics teaching: software' and only four pages on 'Science education'.

The minority who approached the problems of laboratory teaching from a more fundamental, ie educational point of view, concentrated on the matching of aims to methods. This led to a range of innovative teaching methods, many of which upon evaluation demonstrated their superior effectiveness for achieving the aims to which they were matched. Much of this work in the sciences has been reviewed by Boud et al. (1978). From the point of view of the present article, it is significant that the preface to this review states that 'whilst the cost arguments have not yet found a prominent part in the literature of laboratory teaching, a reappraisal of teaching methods is the common theme.'

MATCHING AIMS, METHODS AND ASSESSMENT

Since our own work started in the happier days of the late 1960s, it is not surprising that we too initially ignored the question of cost in our efforts to improve laboratory teaching. Fortunately, however, we were never blessed with riches and nearly always worked within very modest means. So, almost inevitably, increases in effectiveness were also likely to lead to increases in cost-effectiveness. The one exception to this concerned computer assisted learning, of which more will be said later.

The key to our early work was provided by an analysis of the aims of first-year undergraduate physics laboratories (Boud and O'Connell 1970; Boud 1973). This showed that the aims fell broadly into two groups, relating respectively to products and processes. Further, it was found that most of the product aims, eg 'verifying a physical principle', could best be achieved by very short and tightly prescribed laboratory experiences, while most of the process aims, eg 'the acquisition of experimental skills', required considerable freedom in time, procedure and apparatus. Once this was realized, it was also clear that the traditional laboratory experience of three hours of loosely prescribed procedure and apparatus was a compromise which was ill designed to achieve either group of aims. The types of laboratory experience required — 'walk-in' laboratories on the one hand (Price and Brandt 1974) and 'open-ended' experiments on the other (Elton 1966) — were already available, although their significance in terms of laboratory aims had not been recognized. Over the next few years, O'Connell and his co-workers developed both these types of laboratory experience in conjunction with the two groups of aims they were designed to achieve (O'Connell et al. 1977; Kay et al. 1981). It was then found that if the students were explicitly told what the aims were which they were to achieve, they were much more likely to do so.

In retrospect it is interesting that at about the same time the Commission on College Physics (1972) had concluded that there was 'a wide variety of goals which physicists set for the (introductory) laboratory. There seemed little hope of ever making the list of goals converge, and without agreement on goals, how can one reasonably expect to agree on changes in content or style of the laboratory?' Their failure to appreciate that there should be more than one style was and still is shared by the vast majority of university physicists. O'Connell's natural sense of parsimony in both time and money also led him to use very simple and cheap equipment and to exhort students to 'remember that laboratory classes are expensive to run, particularly in terms of staff and student time' (O'Connell 1971). Hence the evaluated achievement of aims was a measure of cost-effectiveness and not merely of effectiveness.

An important feature of the 'walk-in' laboratory was that it was self-instructional, ie students could carry out the appropriate laboratory exercises in it in their own time and without the assistance of supervisory staff. This made it easy to incorporate it in courses that used the Personalized System of Instruction (Keller plan), which until then had only been used to replace lectures (Bridge and Elton 1977, p. 37). The resulting increases in cost-effectiveness were immediately apparent. The self-paced nature of the courses allowed a booking system which enabled students to book a laboratory exercise close to the time when they were studying corresponding subject matter theoretically, something that had never been possible with traditional lecture courses and timetabled laboratory periods. It also made it possible to use a particular piece of laboratory equipment for many more hours in the week and with much less supervision than would have been the case in a traditional set-up. While a cost comparison of Keller plan with the lecture (Unsworth 1978) showed that the former either broke even or was somewhat more expensive, there is little doubt that the inclusion of laboratory work would shift the balance in the opposite direction.

The last point illustrates the fact that the less piecemeal an innovation is, the more capable is it of leading to increases in cost-effectiveness. Thus a more radical innovation, in which the whole of a course — theoretical and practical work — was taught in an integrated way in a learning centre which was a normal classroom (Lopez and Elton 1980), demonstrated not only that students could learn more effectively in this way, but that much of the practical work did not require purpose-built laboratories. An even more interesting finding was that while the course was overtly designed in a rather rigid manner in order to achieve some fairly basic product aims of knowledge and understanding of the subject, the fact that it took place in a learning centre encouraged group work which enabled the students to achieve some much higher level and more general process aims, eg 'to express one's thoughts lucidly both in speech and writing.'

Throughout our work we came up against the problem of assessment and the influence which assessment had on students' attitudes and work. Academic teachers frequently complain that students' learning is directed towards passing examinations and not towards interest in the subject, but if this is so then it implies a gross disparity between the aims which teachers wish their students to achieve and the aims on which they assess them. Attempts by teachers to use exhortation to make students follow teachers' aims rather than assessment aims are usually quite futile. The reason behind this is that 'the spirit and style of student assessment defines the *de facto* curriculum' (Rowntree 1977, p.1) because students simply cannot afford to put their best into work which does not count towards the degree (Elton and Laurillard 1979).

The kind of contradiction indicated in the last paragraph is often at its worst in the laboratory. Dearden (1979) found this in his study of a first-year undergraduate electrical engineering laboratory, as the following brief extract from a group interview indicates:

Interviewer: Are you saying that getting a high mark and understanding the experiment are incompatible?
All: Yes, definitely so.

Student 1:   To get a high mark you must finish the experiment but that doesn't mean you understand it.

The problem arose from the fact that in order to finish the 'experiment' students had to work very fast and this was only possible if they followed the instructions unthinkingly. Thus a 'cookbook' approach, which the teachers explicitly discouraged, was forced on the students by the rules of the assessment. Dearden likens this situation to the 'double bind' syndrome which has been used to explain schizophrenia. While he readily admits that most students do not become mentally ill, he nevertheless makes a strong case for the 'cure' to lie in a change of the environment, ie in the assessment system and not in the student.

The irony of this particular case history is that the department had actually changed the assessment system recently in order to encourage better learning, but had done it in the kind of piecemeal approach which I criticized earlier. Thus marks were awarded for preparation in advance of the laboratory period and this indeed led to such work being done. Another change, to prevent extensive and rather mindless laboratory reports, was that these reports had to be written up briefly during the laboratory period and handed in at the end. On the other hand, the actual laboratory exercises had been left unchanged. The result was the time pressure mentioned earlier. The conclusion which Dearden draws is that the assessment system is indeed a powerful way to influence student learning, but that changes in the system are likely to have unforeseen and equally powerful effects which, if deleterious, must in turn be attended to. While this conclusion may appear blindingly obvious, it must be remembered that it had not been reached by those who ran the laboratory.

Another and very important conclusion which this and similar work leads to is that quite generally an appropriate change in the assessment system may be more effective in improving student learning and at lower cost than anything that can be achieved through an improvement in the teaching skills of individual teachers (Elton 1982).

MATCHING AIMS AND CONTENT
There is a natural tendency for syllabuses to become overloaded as time passes, since it is always easier for a course board to add new material than to persuade its members to withdraw any part of what they are already teaching. To prevent this, it is necessary to insist rigidly that the syllabus must not be enlarged and that content priorities should be established with reference to course aims. This is a difficult exercise, with which course boards at traditional universities are unfamiliar, although it is commonly done by the course teams of the Open University. Experience there indicates that it requires the collaboration of subject specialists and educational technologists.

When such an exercise is undertaken with the intention of increasing cost-effectiveness, then the possibility of syllabus reduction must be considered. If this can be achieved in laboratory work, then the savings in equipment, teaching space, staff time and student time can be substantial. Although the last of these is never costed by administrators, it ought not to be left out of any calculation.

THE USE OF MODERN TECHNICAL DEVELOPMENTS
One of the most successful replacements of the teacher by a machine is the video-recording of demonstrations in the teaching laboratory. In the very common case where a particular experiment is carried out by different students in successive weeks, it is often necessary for the same help and instruction to be given by a hapless

demonstrator, week after week. Watson (1977) lists the following advantages of a video-recording of an experienced lecturer over a live demonstrator:

— It saves staff and demonstrator time.
— It can be of unchanging high quality.
— It offers a flexible service to students.

There are of course disadvantages, such as that a video-tape cannot be interrogated, and some students do find video-recordings impersonal. Overall, however, they have been found acceptable by students and an unforeseen advantage has been that video-tapes have been found useful in familiarizing new demonstrators with their tasks. On the other hand, a rather subtle disadvantage can be that if the performance of the lecturer on the videotape is too nearly perfect, it may depress the students, who cannot hope to emulate him (McConnell 1980).

It is generally estimated that it takes a lecturer one hour to produce one minute of video-tape. When the cost of recording and of media staff is added to this, it becomes clear that it would take many years before the initial cost of playback facilities and the production of video-tapes is balanced against the saving on demonstrators' salaries. Nevertheless, in a careful costing analysis of a major installation in a physiology laboratory (Howland et al. 1975), Fielden and Pearson (1978) concluded that the scheme would break even financially over twelve years and that the unquantifiable educational benefits were significant. In assessing this conclusion, it should be stressed that the scheme was a pioneering venture and that the lessons learned from it (McConnell 1980) should make any repetition of it considerably more cost-effective. Watson (1980) also points out that less traditional forms of laboratory, in which students have more freedom, may find it even more important to have a library of video-taped material which students can use when they require particular help or advice. Finally, the cost of production of video-tapes for a particular institution decreases rapidly if several institutions use the same tape. It is therefore encouraging that Watson (1978) found that about half of a set of chemistry laboratory tapes produced at the University of Sussex could be used at the University of Surrey and that the students' reaction to the tapes was very similar at both universities.

If we now turn to the other major technical development in laboratory work, computer assisted learning (CAL), the situation from the cost point of view is less happy. This is hardly surprising. As an educational aid, the computer is quite radically innovative in a way that is not true of any other technical device. It is highly probable that its educational potential is very much greater than has so far been appreciated and it is likely that greater familiarity with it will bring down the until now very high development costs of educational software. Much of the current educational potential of CAL in the support and replacement of laboratory work can be gathered from the work of McKenzie et al. (1978), and the cost per student hour is estimated by Fielden and Pearson (1978, Ch.13) at £10. The virtue of CAL clearly did not lie in its cost-effectiveness at that time and, although costs have come down, this is still the case. What is, however, also clear is that CAL can lead to kinds of semi-intuitive learning which are immensely valuable in science and engineering and which no other teaching can achieve. The extent to which cost will come down further in the future will depend less on the continuing reduction in hardware costs than on the far less likely reduction in the cost of software production.

TOWARDS CHANGE

It is apparent from the evidence presented that there are ways in which the cost-effectiveness of laboratory work could be increased and that the changes required to produce such increases are rarely at higher than departmental level. The inertia in the system even at this level may be illustrated by the following experience. When I introduced a learning centre (see above, p.102) into the degree course of another department, I removed several three-hour laboratory experiments from the laboratory schedule and replaced them by one-hour self-instructional exercises in the learning centre. This resulted in the lecturer in charge of the laboratory circularizing all his colleagues with a request to develop some new experiments to fill the gaps in the schedule!

If change is to be possible, then time and resources must be made available to generate the change. As regards time, I recommend the ruthlessness of the physics department at Massachusetts Institute of Technology. The staff, having decided that the current first-year laboratory work was ineffective and needed changing, simply cancelled it for one year. During that year the students had no laboratory work while the staff prepared the new work. As regards resources, this may not appear to be an opportune time to ask for minor present expenditures in the expectation of major later savings, but it is likely that the time will become even less opportune in the foreseeable future, while the necessity for saving will increase.

The real obstacles to change lie elsewhere. One is the great rigidity of our present degree structures, often defended in the sacred cause of 'maintaining standards', which allows little freedom to individual teachers and less to students. In such a system, innovation can lead to friction, rivalry and strife. In contrast, the American credit system gives both teachers and students vastly more freedom on the personal scale. This may account at least in part for the much greater incidence of innovation on the other side of the Atlantic.

An even more serious obstacle to change is that there are inadequate incentives in strategically important places. At the level of individual staff it is still true that advancement, if any, is much more likely to come through excellence in research than through teaching. At the next level, that of the department, there is a real disincentive to save in most institutions, since savings are likely to result simply in reduced allocations in future years. An effective arrangement for sharing savings between institution and department has yet to be found. At the same time, the worsening staff/student ratios in most departments may in themselves provide an incentive, since any resources saved by more cost-effective teaching could be used to support the research of the department. At the level of the institution itself, the incentive to save is very real, since the budget of the institution is likely to decrease every year, but the ability to save directly is small. It is therefore perhaps not too much to hope that an institution and its departments, with their de facto largely independent areas of power (Elton 1981), may reach an accommodation of mutual self-interest as indicated above.

Finally, at the highest level, at least as far as the universities are concerned, there is the enigmatic UGC, which on the one hand cuts the budget of each university and on the other resolutely refuses to allow any university to reduce its unit costs. It would be presumptuous for a mere academic to suggest what to do to change the UGC.

CONCLUSION

I have tried to show that the isolated experiences of evaluated innovations indicate that there could be significant improvements in cost-effectiveness, if these innovations were applied more generally. I have also argued that larger improvements could probably follow from an analysis of existing syllabuses in terms of course aims. Finally, I have listed some of the obstacles in the way of improving cost-effectiveness and how they might be overcome. As G.K. Chesterton said about Christianity, it is not that increasing cost-effectiveness has been tried and found difficult, but that it has been found difficult and not tried.

ACKNOWLEDGEMENTS
Although the work reported in this paper is that of many people, the inspiration for nearly all of it came from one person, Mr. S. O'Connell, to whom the rest of us who were involved in it owe much. I also wish to acknowledge here my long-standing debt to Dr. K.G. Britton, senior physics master of Rydal School, Colwyn Bay, who first revealed to me the joys and challenges of laboratory work.

REFERENCES
Boud, D.J. (1973) The laboratory aims questionnaire — a new method for course improvement? *Higher Education* 2, 81-94
Boud, D.J., Dunn, J.G., Kennedy, T. and Walker, M.G. (1978) *Laboratory Teaching in Tertiary Science* Higher Education Research and Development Society of Australasia.
Boud, D.J. and O'Connell, S. (1970) Towards an educational technology of laboratory work *Visual Education* December, 12-13
Bragg, S. (1980). In Evans, N. (Editor) *Education beyond School* London: Grant McIntyre
Bridge, W.A. and Elton, L.R.B. (Editors) (1977) *Individual Study in Undergraduate Science* London: Heinemann Educational Books
Commission on College Physics (1972) *The Divergent Laboratory* University of Maryland
Dearden, G.J. (1979) *Student Learning and Teacher Intervention in an Undergraduate Engineering Laboratory* PhD thesis, University of Surrey
Elton, L.R.B. (1966) New courses at the University of Surrey *Physics Education* 1, 89-96
Elton, L.R.B. (1975) Innovations in undergraduate physics teaching — which and why? *Physics Education* 10, 144-147
Elton, L.R.B. (1981) Can universities change? *Studies in Higher Education* 6, 23-24
Elton, L.R.B. (1982) Assessment for learning. In Bligh, D.A. (Editor) *Professionalism and Flexibility in Learning* Guildford: Society for Research into Higher Education, ch.4
Elton, L.R.B. and Laurillard, D.M. (1978) Trends in research on student learning *Studies in Higher Education* 4, 87-102
Fielden, J. and Pearson, P.K. (1978) *Costing Educational Practice* London: Council for Educational Technology
French, A.P. (1978). In Jones, J.G. and Lewis, J.L. (Editors) *The Role of the Laboratory in Physics Education* International Commission on Physics Education, p. iii
Howland, R.J., Midson, A.J. and Williams, R. (1975) Videotapes in laboratory classes: developments in an integrated approach to physiology teaching *Aspects Educ. Tech.* VIII, 111-120
Kay, S.M., O'Connell, S. and Cryer, P. (1981) Higher level aims in a physics laboratory: a first year course at Royal Holloway College *Studies in Higher Education* 6, 177-184

Lopez, M. and Elton, L.R.B. (1980) A course taught through a learning centre: an evaluation *Studies in Higher Education* 5, 91-99

McConnell, D. (1980) *An Evaluation Study of the Teaching and Learning in a University Human Physiology Laboratory* PhD thesis, University of Surrey

McKenzie, J., Elton, L. and Lewis, R. (Editors) (1978) *Interactive Computer Graphics in Science Teaching* Chichester: Ellis Horwood

O'Connell, S. (1971) Chemical physics: a student designed self-service laboratory course *Student Laboratory Instructions, University of Surrey* Unpublished manuscript

O'Connell, S., Penton, S.J. and Boud, D.J. (1977) A rationally designed self-service laboratory mini-course *J. Prog. Learning and Educ. Tech.* 14, 154-161

Ogborn, J. (Editor) (1977) *Practical Work in Undergraduate Science* London: Heinemann Educational Books

Price, R.M. and Brandt, D. (1974) Walk-in laboratory: a laboratory for introductory physics *American J. Physics* 42, 126-130

Rowntree, D. (1977) *Assessing Students: How shall We know Them?* London: Harper and Row

Unsworth, P. (1978) The Keller Plan: costs and benefits of self paced study. In Piper D.W. (Editor) *The Efficiency and Effectiveness of Teaching in Higher Education* University of London Teaching Methods Unit

Wagner, L. (1982) *The Economics of Educational Media* London: Macmillan.

Watson, J.R. (1977) Videotapes in undergraduate chemistry laboratories *Educ. in Chemistry* 14, 84-86

Watson, J.R. (1980) *A Comparative Study of an Undergraduate Laboratory in Chemistry* PhD thesis, University of Surrey

15 RECESSION AND INNOVATION IN SWEDEN

Staffan Wahlen   *National Board for Universities and Colleges, Stockholm*

Higher education in Sweden is experiencing some of the same hardships that characterize higher education in Britain today. Although in most cases the cuts are not as drastic in Sweden as they are in Britain, and although the structures of the educational systems in the two countries are quite different, similar patterns of consequences develop. Staff reductions become inevitable and affect teaching and research more or less seriously and more or less randomly. Programmes are often pruned not as a result of pedagogical considerations but as a consequence of which teachers choose to go or are forced to resign. The quality of many programmes is affected in terms of staff/student ratio, the number of options open to students, reduced services, the use of obsolete equipment, etc. The relationship between funds and the quality of the end-product, however, is by no means clear, something which has been pointed out by several researchers, eg Harold Bowen, who states that it is tempting to rely on 'the universal tendency to judge institutional results or quality in terms of input ... and to assume without evidence that more resources somehow will inevitably produce commensurately greater or better results. ... There is a serious logical problem, however, in declaring that cost differences are due to differences in program. It is by no means clear whether expensive programs are a result or a cause of high costs' (Bowen, quoted in Kuh 1981, p.13).

In Sweden, budget cuts have affected higher education, and especially research, less than other areas of public expenditure. On average, allocations have been reduced by about four per cent in the last two years. It could also be argued that universities and colleges have not been given sufficient compensation for inflation and that certain types of higher education, notably teacher training programmes, have been more afflicted than others.

Universities and colleges have had their resources diminished in three different ways.

1   Costs per full-time equivalent student (FTE) have been reduced by maintaining the number of students and decreasing allocations.
2   Costs per FTE have been reduced by increasing the number of students with inadequate or no compensation.
3   Student numbers and allocations have been reduced commensurately.

The last of these methods has been used for teacher training programmes, particularly for pre-school teachers, as the need for this category in the next ten-year period is estimated to be lower than was previously prognosticated. The number of places in pre-school teacher training colleges is being cut down at a fairly rapid rate, as Table 15.1 shows.

At the same time some of these colleges have also had their allocations per FTE reduced. As a result, teachers have been made redundant, group sizes have increased, certain subjects have been reduced, and in some cases discontinued. Practical teacher training, which is the most expensive as well as the most important part of the programme, has been reduced, thus making the students less well prepared for their

TABLE 15.1

Year	Number of places available
1980/81	4 758
1981/82	4 614
1982/83	4 005
1983/84	3 600

future careers.

These negative effects can, however, be reinforced or compensated for by other forces. In 1980 entry requirements for this programme were raised appreciably, from nine years' school background to eleven. The combined result of this reform and the lowering of the total number of places available ought to have brought about a higher quality among those admitted. But as the labour market for pre-school teachers has declined, fewer young people have become interested in this highly specialized programme, which will give them limited chances of finding employment as teachers and none outside the teaching profession. The number of applicants has thus dropped significantly (Table 15.2).

TABLE 15.2

Year	No of places available	No of applicants	Ratio
Autumn 1981	1 335	3 489	1:2.6
Autumn 1982	1 287	2 088	1:1.6

Thus, some of the negative pedagogical effects of reduced funding may have been neutralized by the raising of entry requirements. On the other hand, the raising of entry standards may not have yielded the result hoped for as competition for places has become considerably less keen.

Development in other study areas also testifies to the difficulty of isolating resources as a variable when it comes to assessing the quality of a programme. The large age groups of the mid-sixties are now beginning to put pressure on the higher education system in Sweden. To meet the increased demand the government has provided approximately 23,000 new study places for the period 1982-1988, mainly in the fields of science and technology. However, little or no extra money will be allocated for the places, and consequently the allocation per FTE is going to drop. In these fields, too, the labour market is uncertain. Yet it is more 'open' in that it is not restricted to the public sector, nor even restricted to a very specific educational background. The number of applicants has thus gone up at a proportionately quicker rate than the number of places available (Table 15.3).

It seems reasonable to hypothesize that as competition becomes keener, the quality of those admitted becomes higher and that therefore even with smaller

TABLE 15.3

Year		No of places available		No of applicants	Ratio
Autumn 1979	Technology	4 375		5 940	1:1.38
	Physics	340		495	1:1.45
1980	Technology	4 146		6 445	1:1.55
	Physics	340		470	1:1.38
1981	Technology	4 458		8 837	1:1.98
	Physics	340		693	1:2.03
1982	Technology	5 122		10 848	1:2.11
	Physics	369		842	1:2.28

resources the quality of those who graduate may not be lowered.

The negative pedagogical effects of budget cuts may also be compensated for by changes in the curriculum which bring about more effective use of student time. Since the mid-sixties the English Department of Stockholm University has founded its language proficiency teaching programme for first-term students on principles based on those of educational technology. The approach is a structural one, in which the systematic teaching of grammar, vocabulary and pronunciation plays a major role. Put very simply, grammar rules are taught and practised in grammar classes and translation/composition classes. Phonetics and rules of pronunciation are taught in phonetics classes and put into practice in conversation classes. For the acquisition of vocabulary there is a text course consisting of some fifteen works of fiction and non-fiction.

By the early seventies more learner-oriented approaches to language teaching began to develop, especially in Britain and the United States. These take into account the communication needs of the learner and try to systematize the notions that must be able to be expressed in order to be able to communicate. One aspect of this led to the Council of Europe Threshold Level system and the writing of a large variety of textbooks on a notional/functional basis. Another aspect led up to various courses in English for Specific Purposes (see Widdowson 1978; Wilkins 1976). On a more simplistic level it could be added that these approaches also recognize that for purposes of effective communication it is more important to be able to use reasonable stress and intonation patterns than to be able to pronounce the exact variant of a phoneme in a specific variety of English. Modern linguistic research has taken this into consideration when trying to explore language structure on a level above those of phonology, morphology and syntax. Thus the nature of a text, of the paragraph, and the relationships between the elements of a text are now being investigated in text linguistics, and patterns of communication are being examined in discourse analysis (Sinclair and Coulthard 1975).

The developments of language teaching and the findings of the research referred to above were not made use of in the programme of the English Department during the seventies, when allocations and student numbers were relatively stable. However, as the cost per FTE dropped slowly in the latter half of the decade it resulted in the stagnation of teaching methods as slowly increasing groups were allocated fewer hours for each part of the first-term programme.

Funds per FTE dropped more sharply for the academic year 1982/83, and in the spring of 1982 it was proposed to the working groups reviewing the department's programme that rather than continue the cutting of teaching hours allotted to oral proficiency and phonetics for first-term students, and thus making this part of the course meaningless, it was preferable to alter the scope and to focus teaching and testing on effectiveness of communication. It was also proposed that the above-mentioned research should be taken into account when restructuring the course.

A new syllabus was worked out in the early summer and is now being put into effect. Reports so far indicate that the programme is successful, not least because it has contributed to the revitalization of the debate on the relationship between teaching and research.

Three observations can be made on the basis of this case. First, the ideas behind the syllabus change had been in circulation for a considerable period of time, but there had been little interest among the staff in incorporating them in the syllabus or their own teaching. Secondly, far-reaching syllabus changes had been proposed several times in the department's administration, but the proposals had attracted little enthusiasm on the part of the staff. However, the changes described above were in fact mainly worked out by teachers and student representatives. Thirdly, in view of the fact that further cuts were to be expected, complete restructuring seemed a better alternative than the continued gradual reduction of the traditional programme.

Similar reports from other university departments in Sweden indicate that ideas for pedagogical reforms based on research and development may sometimes be put into effect more easily through the pressure of outside negative economic forces which require that offensive measures be taken to solve the problems that arise.

REFERENCES

Kuh, G.D. (1981) *Indices of Quality in the Undergraduate Experience* AAHE-ERIC—Higher Education Research Report No. 4

Sinclair, J.McH. and Coulthard, R.M. (1975) *Towards an Analysis of Discourse* London: Oxford University Press

Widdowson, H. (1978)   *Teaching Language as Communication* London: Oxford University Press

Wilkins, D. (1976) *Notional Syllabuses* London: Oxford University Press

16 THE POTENTIAL OF EDUCATIONAL TECHNOLOGY

Norman Willis   Council for Educational Technology

Even though we are nearing the end of IT82 — a year devoted to a government campaign to increase understanding of the potential, and especially the potential for change, of information technology — it is necessary to reiterate to many educational audiences the fact that technical development in society at large is moving very rapidly and is producing major changes. Much of the public impact of developments in the application of micro-electronics and of the implementation of information technology has been in making ordinary things easier to use, easier to get at, cheaper and more reliable. Students coming forward for higher education know that universities and polytechnics are contributing to the development of these new systems. They are justified in expecting that the teaching and learning methods they encounter will reflect that involvement with the developments they see in commerce, industry and the home: yet they do not. In the report of the House of Commons Education, Science and Arts Committee on the funding and organization of courses in higher education (Education 1980), members said:

'We were impressed by written evidence that educational technology can make a major contribution in reducing costs, improving teaching and changing course patterns. We agree that there will need to be greater use of individualized and distance learning techniques and that information for educational purposes will increasingly be available at home, or at public libraries, and at times convenient to the student. These developments could lead to considerable change of emphasis in the use of capital resources, especially buildings, within higher education. Those responsible for policy decisions in higher education should be aware of educational technology's potential for enabling radical changes and significant savings to be made. We were alarmed that so few of those who gave evidence, including the DES, appeared to appreciate fully that potential.'

Yet in spite of that statement by a powerful committee of the House of Commons, the decisions taken as a result of the reductions in finance imposed on higher education over the past two years have shown no attempt whatever to use the advantages offered by new technology to alleviate or even to overcome those reductions. Higher education has already invested in the provision of facilities for the application of educational technology to its courses. Almost all of the universities, polytechnics and other institutions of higher education have made at least a central appointment and some central provision for an educational technology service: some have made very considerable facilities available. The scale of this provision varies, of course, as a result of a wide range of influences: institutional demand, history, site environment, and the impact of individual personalities. But it can be said with certainty that a great deal of regular use is being made of educational technology, and that it has now become an established feature of the teaching provision in higher education. This current work includes:

— Production of teaching materials in a wide range of media: print, moving picture (both film and television), still picture (slides and overhead projector transparencies), and sound.
— Organization and management of distribution services for equipment and teaching material, including arrangements for the exchange of teaching materials between institutions.
— Provision of advice to, and training for, academic staff in the systematic structuring and design of teaching materials to achieve stated ends, and direct involvement in teams producing such structured materials.
— Co-operation in the development of innovative teaching strategies, especially in respect of systems for individualized instruction and schemes for 'open' or 'distant' learning (including assistance to students in acquiring the necessary study skills).

In addition to this work carried out by central service units (CSU) and educational development units (EDU), higher education has also developed considerable experience in computer-assisted learning (largely as a result of the five-year National Development Programme in Computer Assisted Learning which ended in December 1977 (Hooper 1977). This work has in the main developed within subject departments, rather than through the agency of the institution's CSU or EDU. The senior staff of CSUs and EDUs, together with those responsible for computer assisted learning, represent a large proportion of the leadership of professional educational technologists in the United Kingdom.

Yet the potential of this investment (together with that in libraries and central computing services, all of which are complementary as a recent CET investigation has made plain (Collier 1981)) for the positive alleviation of the present situation has not only been ignored, the central services have been singled out in many cases for disproportionate cuts. The base upon which an innovative restructuring of the teaching methods and institutional structures of higher education might be built is being eroded before any attempt has been made to analyse ways in which new technology can be used to support radical change.

One reason for this undoubtedly stems from the frequently expressed view that the use of educational technology has tended to 'improve quality without reducing cost'. This judgement is quite fair, so long as it relates to past practices, where various resources have been used to extend or improve an existing teaching method: in these circumstances the use of educational technology and the time spent in preparing teaching materials in different media represent an 'add-on' cost. However, there is now evidence (Birch and Cuthbert 1981; Fielden and Pearson 1978) that, if a department or institution is prepared to modify its teaching system, new teaching techniques can at least match existing costs and in some cases effect positive economies. Techniques for costing educational practices have been developed by CET which enable the costs both of 'traditional' methods of teaching and of innovative methods to be expressed in terms which permit their varying contribution to be assessed. These techniques undoubtedly need to be refined and developed, but, given the will, it is now possible to cost out the implications of changes in teaching techniques.

The system at present contains some expensive practices which could be rationalized. In the production of teaching materials by individual institutions expensive academic time and specialized production capacity are expended within an institution in creating learning materials, sometimes of considerable complexity, for a course which is largely similar to that in other institutions throughout the country. Yet such materials are rarely used elsewhere because of minor course variations or, more likely, because of sheer unwillingness to use materials from a 'rival' institution. Whilst recognizing immediately the need for variety of approach, and the dangers of ossifying the teaching of a subject by the use of mass-produced material, nevertheless the cost to higher education of the 'not-invented-here' syndrome is high and should be recognized, particularly in the present economic climate. Indeed, institutions should be giving concentrated attention to the possibility of squeezing even more value out of these materials by marketing them both in the UK and overseas in order to provide extra revenue. Potential markets will be created by the establishment of the Open Tech and by the PICKUP programme of continuing education. Channel 4, recently opened, can provide a market for specialized, high-quality television programmes from higher education institutions and, in addition, complete recorded courses can be offered for sale in video-cassette form for professional updating and improvement (as is already done by several universities in the United States — an initiative being followed by some universities in Britain). Such revenue-earning activities, of course, require the support of an efficient service organization which most institutions are not set up to provide, but there is no reason why institutions should not collaborate to support an 'Enterprises' company — or indeed make appropriate marketing arrangements with existing commercial concerns. In either case, the institution's educational technology unit will need to collaborate closely with academic departments to ensure that the materials produced are to an appropriate standard for wide distribution.

Supported self-study, using high-quality materials specially designed for their purpose, seems likely to be able to provide a way of coping with many of the immediate problems caused by the cuts in higher education. For example, as staff numbers are reduced in a particular academic area or as courses are phased out and staff numbers have to be run down in advance of completion of a course, severe problems arise in maintaining coverage of the curriculum. This problem is aggravated by the use of premature retirement schemes which, although avoiding possible redundancies, ensure that the vacancies arising are randomly scattered. Here is a problem which can be directly eased by the use of self-study materials, whether developed within the institution or shared between institutions (Lewis 1981a). Such materials could well be distributed — in whole or in part — by the new communications media, because the combination of developments in telecommunications, video and computing has provided the basis for the creation of new powerful electronic information and communications systems. The potential impact of this 'information technology' on our lives is such that some commentators have spoken of it in terms of a 'revolution'.

In considering its implications for education the Council for Educational Technology (CET) understands information technology to consist of three main elements:

— Information Handling — the storage and retrieval of information.
— Communications Technology — the transmission of information.
— Information Transformation — the manipulation of information; putting it
  into a form in which it is usable for a particular purpose.

The power of information technology derives from these three elements used in combination. The role of the library, the application of computers, the use of radio,

TV and other AV media, and even the college telephone, are all facets of information technology in education. Indeed the Council is currently investigating all potential aspects of videotex, particularly those offered by Prestel; the distribution of educational computer programmes by telesoftware; electronic publishing; teleconferencing; interactive video; and a possible educational environment for the 1990s.

Here CET's concern is not only with the application of individual technologies, but also with the implications for education, both beneficial and detrimental, resulting from their convergence. This impact, together with decreasing costs and increasing reliability are major factors enabling the creation of an educational equivalent of the electronic office. The Council is initiating a public debate on the implications and consequences of the convergence of these technologies for education in the medium to long term, which will throw up possible policies and strategies for educational development in the 1990s. Underlying all this development work is an awareness that the needs and interests of the educational user must be paramount — advice and guidance on the successful integration of the technologies into existing teaching methods is as important as the development of new opportunities and ways of learning. For these new techniques, especially in the areas of telecommunications and information handling, will make it increasingly possible for students to carry out the 'information gathering' aspects of their courses at home, or at places much nearer their home than a university or college (for example, in public libraries) and at times convenient to the student rather than to the educational institution.

This does not, of course, overcome the need for seminar and tutorial work — the essential core of higher education where the student is able to test newly gained ideas against a highly trained mind; quite the reverse. But such developments, where the number of students living on campus, or the length of time they spend within the institution, may be reduced considerably, would lead to a considerable change of emphasis in the use of capital resources, and particularly the stock of buildings, within higher education. Over recent years, progress has been made, by several different organizations, in the development of open and individualized learning techniques, especially in course design, distribution and production (Lewis and Jones 1980), in tutor training (Lewis 1981b), in course organization and administration; and in the recognition, if not solution, of problems experienced by students. Much of this work is being co-ordinated by the Council in its 'open learning systems' programme which, although designed specifically for non-advanced further education students, is providing experience which could readily be transferred to higher education.

Changes of so radical a nature must be supported first by changes in the approach to planning in higher education. There is now widespread expression of the need for better planning. The DES has said that 'a more structured approach may be needed to the identification of new needs ... in terms of academic balance and objectives' and the Committee of Directors of Polytechnics (CDP) has commented that 'a mechanism must be found to establish priorities and to plan higher education as a whole.' Educational technology is based upon the need for systematic analysis of educational requirements and course provision, the setting of clear objectives, and the evaluation of the results achieved. Yet throughout higher education this expertise is not being applied to *planned* efforts to ensure that the nation at large is given the flexible education system it needs for the production of specialists, the creation of awareness and the maintenance of personal self-esteem. It is little short of a tragedy that the contribution of technology and educational technologists to improving the capacity and quality of higher education is not being given consideration at the highest level.

Second, there need to be changes in the training of lecturers and other staff to meet radical changes in teaching methods and teachers' roles. There is little doubt that some past failures in the application of educational technology can be traced to the introduction of new technology without adequate effort being made to train the lecturing staff who were to be involved. As things stand at present in higher education, improvement of teaching technique is a marginal, rather than a central, preoccupation. Therefore, if advances in educational technology are to play their full part in higher education, there will need to be an effort towards staff reorientation, not merely in teaching techniques but also in attitudes towards priorities and status, which is far in excess of the modest impetus towards staff development currently being provided by staff development and learning methods units. Reorientation on the scale required is unlikely to be achieved by the imposition of solutions by 'outsiders'. It is far more likely to be successful if it can proceed through the co-operative involvement of the lecturing staff themselves, under the encouragement of a firm institutional commitment and understanding of the need for change.

The effective application of teaching techniques which make considerable use of equipment in their 'delivery' systems also requires that adequate numbers of properly trained non-teaching support staff are employed. At a time of severe restriction of funds it is important that disproportionate reductions are not imposed on essential maintenance and operative services. Too often existing systems are blamed for mechanical failures when quite inadequate provision has been made for support services. In this regard, CET has noted the pre-eminence of polytechnics in providing educational development units which combine work in educational technology with continuing programmes of development in teaching technique for the staff of the institution. We regret that this movement is not paralleled in the universities.

Changes in training need to be supported by changes in attitudes, especially attitudes towards the recognition of the value of various types of work carried out by teaching staff. From the point of view of the individual member of staff of an institution, there is little advantage to be gained by devoting time and effort to the development and adoption of innovative teaching methods, beyond the personal satisfaction of knowing that student achievement is being improved. This is because career advancement has tended, historically, to depend upon success in research work and publication. Whilst there is now agreement that good teaching performance is also taken into consideration, no recognition for promotion purposes is given to the investment of time in course design and the development of teaching materials. Yet such work is at least as intellectually demanding as other forms of research work and the preparation of books for publication.

Third, there needs to be a completely different institutional attitude to the acceptability of change. At present, there is little incentive to introduce changes of teaching method in higher education. The 'power' of a department is measured at least as much by size of budget and number of staff and students as by academic standing. A reduction of budgetary need or of staff requirement by introducing new techniques may well be seen as a threat, not as a benefit. Where savings are currently being made as a result of innovative practices, they tend to be masked by a shift of resources to, for example, research or more student contact, both of which may well be very desirable ends. An overt decision is therefore required on what the aim of such changes should be, otherwise innovative practices may be criticized for failing to achieve an aim which had never been set.

The general lack of attention to the potential of educational technology, at the highest policy-making levels in higher education, is a brake upon the full application of the new teaching and learning methods which are now, and will increasingly in the future, be available. Whatever the outcome of the current discussions, the new technology will only be able to play a full part in meeting the needs of higher education if action is taken to:

— Provide guidance from the centre (perhaps at government level) on the need to employ the methods made available by technological developments, and the expected benefits of doing so.
— Ensure full institutional commitment to the introduction of new methods.
— Plan adequately and openly and set clear aims to be achieved by the institution or department through the introduction of new methods.
— Make systematic improvement of teaching method, an activity which yields worthwhile rewards to those involved.

At a time when major policy decisions are being taken which will affect the direction of higher education beyond the end of this century, it is essential that those who are responsible for such decisions in higher education should be alive to the potential which existing, and immediately forthcoming, developments in educational technology have for enabling radical changes to be made in the structure of the whole system.

REFERENCES

Birch, D.W. and Cuthbert,R.E. (1981) *Costing Open Learning in Further Education* London: Council for Educational Technology

Collier, G. (1981). In Willis, N. (Editor) *Teaching and Learning Support Services, I: Higher Education* London: Council for Educational Technology

Education Science & Arts Committee (1980) *Funding and Organization of Courses in Higher Education, Vol I, para 117* House of Commons, Fifth Report Session 1979-80. London: HMSO

Fielden, J. and Pearson, P.K. (1978) *Costing Educational Practice* London: Council for Educational Technology

Hooper, R. (1977) *National Development Programme on Computer Assisted Learning* London: Council for Educational Technology

Lewis, R. (1981). *How to Write Self-Study Materials* London: Council for Educational Technology

Lewis, R. (1981) *How to Tutor on an Open Learning Scheme* (self-study version) London: Council for Educational Technology

Lewis, R. and Jones, G. (Editors) (1980) *How to Write a Distance Learning Course: a self-study pack for authors* London: Council for Educational Technology

17 TECHNOLOGY AND THE RESOURCES PARADOX

Nick Rushby   Imperial College, London

As education moves further into the 1980s it is being assailed both by the general recession and by information technology. We might regard each of these as a threat or as a challenge — certainly both of them will have a considerable impact on our education system. The interaction of these two pressures brings with it several paradoxes and dilemmas. The resolution of the resultant problems is beyond our scope here but it is realistic to air the problems in the hope of provoking discussion.

THE RESOURCES PARADOX

Over the past few years there has been a major change in the rules of the innovation game. Although it is difficult to identify a precise date, there has been a distinct change of policy in the public aims of education. Prior to about 1980, resources in the form of institutional commitment and external funding were directed to the support of innovation which was aimed at improving the *quality* of education. It was accepted that the cost of education might increase, but this could be justified by the increased benefits. Now, with the recession and an apparent devaluation of education, it seems that society requires a reduction in the *costs* of education and is prepared to accept that quality may suffer in consequence. The focus of innovation has shifted to the cost components in the cost-benefit equation, and is requiring us to refocus our attention on ideas and developments which might help us to achieve these new aims. Simultaneously, the range of techniques available to us has been increased by the emergence of the new technology of communications and information processing. Education is largely concerned with communications and the acquisition of information, and much of the new technology could be applied to our activities. Some of it might improve our cost-effectiveness, or be used to minimize the unpleasant consequences of recession.

Unfortunately, almost all innovation, whether it is aimed at improving effectiveness or at reducing costs, initially requires additional resources over and above those needed to operate the present system, for research, development, and implementation. In order to save resources in the long term it is necessary to provide more resources in the short term. The grass may indeed be greener on the far side of the hill, but first we must climb over the summit. It is paradoxical that we are inhibited from making more use of information technology to help us through the recession, because of that recession.

THE CURRICULUM-APPLICATION PARADOX

Ever since that fateful evening when the BBC screened their documentary programme 'Now the Chips are Down' there has been a remarkable pressure on education to introduce students at all levels to information technology. The effect on the UK education system can be likened to the American response to the first Soviet sputnik! Funding programmes have abounded, institutions and individuals have responded with courses of various types on information technology, micro-electronics, and programming. Comparisons are continually drawn with efforts in other countries to highlight areas where we might be lagging behind, and strenuous efforts are made to ensure that we offer the best. Yet, among all this activity there is a suspicion of 'do what I say — not what I do.' Academics, even including those teaching information technology, are being very slow to take advantage of their new opportunities. Why is this?

We can identify a number of reasons, most of which are familiar to those involved in innovation. We have already noted the problem of finding adequate resources in a time of recession — a problem which is more acute when part of those resources must go towards *teaching about* rather than *teaching with the aid of* information technology. There is the problem of the inservice training of teachers to use new techniques (there is *the* problem of inservice — and preservice — training for teachers in higher education, but that is another story), and the inherent inertia of the education system and protracted timescale of any change. There is an urgency about the information technology revolution that is expressed in graphs which show that the rate of change — of falling costs, rising speeds, increased power to store, process and transmit information — is doubling every few years. Because this is exciting, it leads to an expectation that its use should also increase at the same dizzy rate. As innovators we must acknowledge that this is unlikely and probably undesirable. The introduction of information technology into education is not being inhibited by technological problems: by and large it is already possible to do anything we want to do with the technology that already exists. Rather, it is limited by our inability to make effective and appropriate use of what technology we already have at our disposal. Perhaps we are expecting too much and too soon of the new revolution?

The business of education is ultimately concerned with information, and so it would seem that new ways of handling information more efficiently and effectively would help to reduce the resources needed and enable the system to cope better with recession. Information technology can help the teacher to prepare his materials more easily, can help communication between teacher and student, and can help the student to learn. By taking over some of the routine tasks in the teaching learning process it can leave both teacher and student more time to concentrate on those aspects which need human intelligence. In practice the situation is more complicated. The possibilities of information technology are sufficiently large to change our aims and expectations, and other factors limit the gains that can be realized. To illustrate some of these complexities, we shall consider four examples of information technology in higher education.

WORD PROCESSING
With the proliferation of micro-computers and suitable software, an increasing number of teachers have access to word processors for the preparation of student handouts, papers, and manuscripts for their books. Since revisions can be made easily, without the labour of retyping or of cut and paste, the resources needed to correct and update printed material can be substantially reduced. In many institutions, access to a word processor may be the only practical way of coping with unfilled and frozen secretarial vacancies, although it is not clear whether it really is cheaper to ask teachers to do their own typing, albeit with technological help. Once over the initial learning period, using a word processor is seductively easy. Typographical errors are easily corrected and the author can soon arrive at the equivalent of a copy-typed document. But the author can then take the opportunity of improving on earlier drafts and the potential savings are traded for the pursuit of perfection.

However, there are some real savings to be found. Papers, conference proceedings and monographs produced on word processors can be published from camera ready copy as a cheaper alternative to typesetting, thus cutting the costs of academic publishing. Student handouts can be tailored for specific courses and made more concise. There is also some subjective evidence that students take more care with well produced handouts and are less likely to use spare copies as scrap paper. One institution is now starting to use a phototypesetter to produce the masters for student handouts. The resulting material is more compact, is thus cheaper to copy, and is even more highly valued by the students.

TELECONFERENCING

The technology of teleconferencing is not startling. Instead of the traditional mode of telephone calls involving two people in a private conversation, a number of people in different physical locations are all connected together via a common telephone link and can participate in a group discussion. Our experience of this simple technique is limited, but it does seem to offer a much cheaper alternative to some meetings where the participants would otherwise have to travel into order to conduct their joint business. Thus, for example, professional meetings involving colleagues from different institutions can be cheaper, and group tutorials in open learning schemes can become feasible. The visible costs of travel and subsistence are forcing us to economize on such meetings: the hidden costs of travelling time aggravate our difficulties.

There are also some new problems. Although the total costs of teleconferencing are less than for face to face meetings, the fall in the travel and subsistence budget is partly compensated by a rise in telephone charges. Where these two items fall under the control of different authorities, teleconferencing may be unwelcome to those responsible for the telephone bill.

The second problem which becomes apparent the first time one experiences a teleconference is that the techniques for effective participation are rather different and it is necessary to adjust one's working habits. Papers must be circulated and studied in advance; communication is by voice only, so there are no visual cues or clues as to the reaction of other participants; the role of the chairman is crucial and a stricter sense of discipline is needed. While the new skills for effective teleconferencing may be acquired by experience, we might consider helping the process by including them in staff development courses.

INFORMATION RETRIEVAL

The number and size of databases accessible and of use to both teachers and their students is slowly increasing. Again, the use of database systems tends to bring new ways of working and organizing personal information, so that significant savings are only realized after some adjustment. It may no longer be necessary to maintain personal card indexes if bibliographic data are readily available through a terminal on, or close to, your desk.

As the costs of information retrieval fall and access becomes more open, we might encourage students to make greater use of the systems, so reducing their dependence on teachers to provide comprehensive reading lists. Of course, they would need to acquire the skills of accessing database systems early on in their courses and the possible savings in time and effort might be cancelled out by the additional teaching needed. There is also the probability that the same amount of time as before would be devoted to information retrieval and that the net result would be more information, rather than resource savings.

COMPUTER BASED LEARNING

There is a growing literature on the introduction of computer based learning (see References). These also discuss the potential savings to be made, for example, in reduced learning time or in simulating expensive learning experiences. It is, or can be, a comprehensive application of information technology to education, involving the storage and transmission of large amounts of information mediated by the computer, which acts as a tutor, referee, laboratory or manager, taking on one or several roles at any time. It can be employed either as a 'small' or as a 'big' medium, and brings with it many of the general problems of educational innovation. It also highlights the specific problems we have discussed in looking at word processing, teleconferencing and information retrieval.

First, there is the problem of change of role for both the teacher and the student. The ways in which we teach and in which we learn are different in a computer based learning environment. The teacher may spend less time in transmitting knowledge but will spend more time in preparing course materials and in a facilitating, tutorial role. The student is forced away from a passive, towards an active participation in his learning and is often required to take more responsibility. He may be unable or unwilling to cope with this. To what extent can students be expected to read for degrees instead of being taught? The overall consequence may be that, after the initial euphoria, courses become static and students become disenchanted. Economies will have been achieved — but at the cost of learning.

Secondly, there is the problem of our attitude to the aims of innovation. We are reluctant to make changes to accommodate the effects of cutbacks and, as committed teachers, would much rather trade these off against improved learning for our students. It is an attitude which is difficult to criticize when the noble pursuit of learning is set against the crude reality of recession. Thirdly, there is the problem of moving resources from one budget to another. Education is traditionally very labour intensive, with a relatively large recurrent budget. Computer based learning, together with the other techniques we have discussed, requires more capital investment for staff development, equipment, and preparation of materials, in order to make longer term savings. In a time of recession, that capital investment is not easily found and administrations are reluctant to vire resources from one budget to another.

CONCLUSION

Workers in some industries are concerned that the use of information technology is threatening their job security and their quality of life. There are few who would argue that this is the case in education. There is no real evidence that teachers can sensibly be replaced by the new technologies, even if this were considered desirable. Instead, if it can be introduced appropriately, information technology can help us to make savings in other areas and so *preserve* salary budgets. Educational innovation was once likened to 'moving the deckchairs on the Titanic from port to starboard': information technology within and outside educaiton may well alter our relationship with the iceberg, but it will take time.

REFERENCES

Fielden, J. and Pearson, P.K. (1977) *The Cost of Learning with Computers* London: Council for Educational Technology

House, E.R. (1974) *The Politics of Educational Innovation* Berkeley: McCutchon

122   Rushby

McDonald, B. et al. (1977) The educational evaluation of NDPCAL *British Journal of Educational Technology* 8 (3)

Rushby, N.J. (1981) Educational innovation and computer based learning. In Rushby, N.J. (Editor) *Selected Readings in Computer Based Learning* London: Kogan Page

Conclusion

18 THREE INNOVATION STRATEGIES

Geoffrey Squires   University of Hull

It is not easy to sum up the deliberations of some seventy people over three days, particularly when most of those deliberations took place in small groups, and when the conference papers tended to be used obliquely rather than directly. Nevertheless an attempt must be made, and the comments will be organized under three broad headings: the attitude to the recession; the types of innovation; and the process of innovation. Since the conference did not attempt to define innovation in any precise terms, neither will we.

The ambiguities of members' attitudes towards the current situation in higher education were neatly caught in the conference title. Was it innovation during recession? Innovation despite recession? Innovation because of recession? Many of the negative effects of recession were of course commented on in discussion: the restrictions on access; the low morale of staff; the pressure on students to go for 'surface' learning; the institutional emphasis on retrenchment; the erosion of consensual or collegial processes; and so on. Yet there was also the recognition that the recession provided, or could provide, a challenge;that it could, in some cases, be turned to positive effect. More than one member noted that the great period of expansion in higher education in the 1960s and 1970s had not brought with it a concomitant increase in innovation, and that perhaps, paradoxically, a time of contraction might produce more departures from traditional norms, structures and practices. Some suggested that the Society for Research into Higher Education (SRHE) might be a midwife, or at least have an attendant role to play, in relation to such changes. The mood of the conference, therefore, was by no means purely a defensive or self-pitying one; there was a good deal of determination to see what could be done, even in difficult circumstances.

What could be done was pointed to in the various papers. Many of the types or directions of innovation discussed in the papers found their way, albeit a little indirectly, into the final reports of the sub-groups, and the comments of members at the concluding plenary session. The range of possible innovations was wide, and bore on every aspect of higher education: the need to use students as a resource; the need to market courses more systematically;the encouragement of credit systems and credit transfer; the use of project work; the emphasis on continuing and post-experience education; the need to attend to staff energy, morale, stress and career development; the diffusion of educational research and innovation; the development of new teaching methods; the utilization of technology; the development of study skills; the setting-up of experimental institutions; education for capability; and more. There was no shortage of ideas, and even a good deal of consensus about the types or kinds of innovation that might be appropriate in the present circumstances. Clearly, 'appropriateness' would depend on local, and indeed national circumstances; the conference was providing a range of possibilities rather than a prescribed solution. Clearly, also, some innovations were potentially double-edged in these difficult days; evaluation could be used to terminate courses and axe jobs; new technology could be used to undercut face-to-face teaching; marketing could lead to distortion; over-responsiveness to loss of academic integrity. Such dangers were well-recognized by the conference, and taken into account, but they did not halt the search for appropriate types of innovation.

It was however, the third aspect of the discussions — the process of innovation — which proved the most intractable and perhaps the most interesting. As several speakers pointed out, good ideas, even when backed by substantial research, do not automatically get implemented. How then, does innovation come about? Or to put it negatively and perhaps more realistically, why does it not come about more often than it does? Here, a major difference of approach opened up in the final plenary session, with some speakers arguing for planned innovation, involving formal and perhaps centralized structures, and others arguing for individual incentives. The former had an image of the dynamic agency; the second an image of the entrepreneurial lecturer. The former invoked something like a higher education council, together with experimental institutions, reserve funds, and systematic research development and diffusion, involving staff developers. The latter concentrated on removing obstacles to, and providing incentives for, individual academics, so that they could unleash their natural urge to innovate.

Clearly, this is to over-simplify the discussion, and the situation. Strategies of innovation are contingent upon the nature of the organization in question, and in particular upon the nature and distribution of power and control within it. One would not expect to find much 'top-down' innovation in a very decentralized or devolved organization; neither would one be likely to come upon much 'bottom-up' innovation in a highly authoritarian or centralized one. Before we can decide whether top-down or bottom-up innovation is more likely to succeed in higher education, we must first decide what kind of organization higher education is; and here lies the real problem.

At the lowest level, it is clear that individual lecturers still have a good deal of autonomy in certain aspects of their work, particularly in terms of research, course planning, teaching, and to a lesser extent assessment. Professional and collegial norms tend to underwrite this autonomy. The entrepreneurial or active lecturer can do a good deal on his or her own. Where three or four such people come together, one gets a small hive of innovation; and if they have the support of their immediate colleagues and head of department, one has that recognizable phenomenon, the lively department. Personal relationships are important in this, but also to some extent unplannable, and often transient, since innovators have a habit of moving on. All this would seem to point towards a 'bottom-up' model of innovation in higher education, with consequent emphasis on minimizing obstacles and providing incentives for individuals, in terms of time, money and regulations.

At the other end of the scale, it is clear that central bodies can have, and have had a major impact on higher education in the last decade and more, for better for worse. DES, UGC, CNAA and now the NAB have been in a position to make major reorientations of policy, the effects of which have permeated right down to individual teaching and learning.

The creation of the Open University, the UGC's new blood scheme, the process of course validation, and the development of credit transfer, are only four examples of 'top-down' initiatives which have affected the whole fabric of higher education in this country. (Conference members from Sweden and Holland cited parallel examples.) In some cases the levers of control have been financial, in others statutory, in others again a combination of the two. In the UK, we have found that the system is more centralized than we thought it was; and there are signs that it may become even more so in* years to come, with moves towards transbinary rationalization, and possible changes in the funding of research. Could not the centralized powers of the system then be used to encourage and promote innovation, assuming that innovation is what most academics would see as change for the better? One group at the conference recommended that the UGC/DES should reserve 2½% of the total funds available for higher education in the next two decades to set up a number of experimental institutions to pioneer changes leading to more flexible structures, more open curricula, increased use of technology and greater cost-effectiveness. Could some central development body, drawing perhaps on SRHE expertise, play a part in such planned innovation? There are, thus, strong arguments in favour of a top-down strategy, arguments which imply agencies with much more muscle than the Schools Council (which the 'bottom-up' exponents used as one among several examples of failed centralized initiatives).

If bottom-up innovation, in terms of individual lecturers, and top-down innovations, in terms of central bodies, can both be argued for plausibly, where does this leave departments and institutions? Are they simply caught in the middle, between the demands and initiatives of their members and the fiats of the authorities? Are they essentially reactive, rather than active? How far can they innovate, as distinct from facilitate, or acquiesce in, innovation? How far can institutions develop any corporate direction or momentum, as distinct from refereeing the competing demands of their departments; or at least minimizing conflicts between them? These are perhaps the most difficult questions of all about innovation in higher education, and the comments of some members suggested the need for both institutions and their constituent departments to engage in corporate planning, on a regular, systematic and medium-term (three to five year) basis. Such a notion sends us back to the middle group of papers on innovations in institutions (Chapters 7-12 in this volume) which relate to marketing, evaluation, course planning, and the auditing and development of staff resources. The difficulties that attend such corporate planning are great: the ambiguous and sometimes ineffable goals of higher education; the anarchic habits of some staff; the absence of consensus on many issues; the difficulty of measuring anything; the fluidity of circumstances; and so on. Such difficulties have been encountered, but also surmounted in some institutions which have tried to plan in a systematic way. Such institutions develop, over a period of time, a characteristic identity, or to use the American term, mission. Since they cannot stand for everything, they stand for something; and this identity then makes it easier for them to decide on priorities right down the line. It has also the side-effect, perhaps welcome, of providing greater obvious diversity in higher education; 'perhaps' because diversity may also be associated with differences in status.

The implications of this analysis of the process of innovation (as distinct from the direction or type of innovation) are that a three-pronged approach is needed. Individual lecturers need to be given scope and incentives to innovate; departments and institutions need to engage in some form of corporate, forward planning; and central bodies should give financial and structural support to experiment and development. Neither 'bottom-up' nor 'top-down' is going to be enough on its own; and the middle must establish its own direction and momentum. Whether these three strategies of innovation would reinforce each other, or conflict with each other, is an interesting question, and one that the conference did not, unfortunately, have time to resolve.